Organize Your Life and More

Save Time and Money, Reduce Stress, Remove Clutter

by

Christina Scalise

Published by
Brighton Publishing LLC
501 W. Ray Road
Chandler, AZ 85225

Organize Your Life and More

Save Time and Money, Reduce Stress, Remove Clutter

by

Christina Scalise

Published by
Brighton Publishing LLC
501 W. Ray Road
Suite 4
Chandler, AZ 85225
BrightonPublishing.com

Copyright © 2012

ISBN 13: 978-1-621830-05-4
ISBN 10: 1-621-83005-5

Printed in the United States of America

First Edition

Cover Design By: Tom Rodriguez

Acknowledgements

I would like to extend my heartfelt thanks to all my family and friends for their patience and encouragement while writing this book. To my husband; thank you for your love, support, and understanding. To my sons; thank you for your contributions and opinions. And a special thank you to my daughter, Jessica Scalise, for all her help and hard work. Great job, Jessica!

To my mother, for her words of wisdom; and my father, whose words of wisdom are still with me today—I thank you both.

And to my sisters and friends who contributed their opinions, I am also thankful.

In addition, I would also like to thank the staff at Brighton Publishing. Your hard work and dedication to making this book a success is very much appreciated!

Table of Contents

Introduction

Chapter One
Why Organize?

Chapter Two
Some Things to Keep in Mind While Organizing

1) The ABC's of Organization

2) Realistic Organization

3) Sometimes Less Really Is More

4) A Place for Everything and Everything in Its Place

5) Don't Try to Do it All at Once

6) Different Ways to Organize

7) Using Spreadsheets to Organize Your Information

8) Sometimes You Need to Make a Bigger Mess to Achieve Less Mess

9) Make it Work for You

10) Family Members

11) Labels

12) Success=Organization & Organization=Success

Chapter Three
Finding Ambition & Avoiding Interruptions

1) Remember Why

2) Focus on Areas of the Greatest Concern

3) Make Cleaning and Organizing Fun

4) January is National Organizing Month

5) Fighting Procrastination

6) Learn to Say No

7) The "To Do" List

8) Pick a Number and Challenge Yourself

9) Five Minutes

10) Avoid Interruptions to Get the Job Done

11) No More Excuses

Chapter Four
Getting Help

1) Help Wanted

2) How to Get Your Kids to Help With Household Chores

3) How to Get Help Doing the Laundry

4) If You Want Something Done, Ask a Busy Person to Do It

Chapter Five
Organizing Products

1) Label Makers

2) Clear Containers Are Best For Storing Items Away

3) Square vs. Round

4) Adjustable Shelving

Chapter Six
How to Store Your Items

1) Categorize Before You Organize

2) Keep It Stored Vertically

3) Stack and Store Vertically or Horizontally to Save Room

4) Make It Stand Out With Colors

5) Alphabetize or Sort By Size and Color

6) Save the Small Stuff

7) What To Store In Fireproof Containers or Safety Deposit Box

8) Empty Containers and Lids

9) Visualize to Organize: See it, Find It

10) Pegboards

Chapter Seven
Where to Store Your Items

1) Creative Storage

2) Wasted Spaces

3) Hidden Storage Hiding in Your Cabinets

4) Store Away for Future Use

5) Within Reach

6) Store Regularly Used Items Within Reach of Children

Chapter Eight
Clutter Control

1) General Rules to Controlling Clutter Before It Starts

2) Temporary Clutter

3) "I Have Too Much Stuff!"

4) Get-Rid-Of Pile

5) Discard Baskets

6) How to Plan a Garage Sale

7) How to Organize a Junk Drawer

8) Sentimental Belongings

9) How Many Can You Get Rid Of?

Chapter Nine
How to Remember What You Always Forget

1) Don't Forget

2) Where to Write It Down

3) Create a Set of Instructions to Avoid Saying or Hearing These Words: "I Can't Remember How to Do That; I Will Figure It Out Later!"

4) "I Can't Remember Where I Put It!"

5) Remember to Pay Those Bills on Time!

6) Index Card Reminders

7) To Do List at Work

Chapter Ten
Time

1) Guilt

2) Multitasking and Saving Time

3) Schedule It In

4) Timesharing

5) Individualize

6) Save Computer Time

Chapter Eleven
Plan Ahead

1) Family Calendar

2) Be Prepared and Stock Up

3) Gift Ideas and Preparation

4) Trip Lists

5) Emergency Kits

6) Final Affairs in Order

7) Death of a Loved One

8) A Great Quote to Remember

Chapter Twelve
Finances

1) Designate an Area for Bill Paying

2) Check All Statements Thoroughly

3) Tax Receipts

4) Too Many Accounts

Chapter Thirteen
Paperwork

1) Eight Ways to Reduce or Eliminate Those Piles of Papers

2) Questions to Ask Yourself Before Throwing Away Papers

3) What and When to Toss

4) Double Up Your Filing System

5) Computer Folders

6) How to Keep up With Incoming Mail

7) Make Time to Read Those Articles

8) Finding Your Receipts

9) Storage of Your Pending Receipts

10) Tackle That Drawer Full of Papers

11) Highlight and Bold

Chapter Fourteen
Family Communication

1) Post Important Information Where It Is Needed Most

2) Dinner Time

3) Information for Each Folder

Chapter Fifteen
Organizing Your Kids

1) Twenty Ways to Get Your Child to Pick Up and Organize Their Bedroom—and Keep It That Way

2) Chore Sheets

3) Job Cards for Kids

4) Rule Sheets

5) Jobs List for Kids

6) Have a "Fun Things to Do" List Ready to Go

7) Leaving Your Children Home Alone

8) Back to School

9) Don't Forget the Homework

10) Planning for the Future

11) Preparing for College

12) Leaving for College

Chapter Sixteen
In the Closet

1) Separate Clothing

2) Briefly Worn Clothing

3) How to Organize a Closet and Quickly Determine Which Clothes to Get Rid Of

Chapter Seventeen
Gardening

1) Springtime Planting

2) Garden Layout

3) Plant Progress

Chapter Eighteen
Shopping

1) Extra Long Shopping Lists

2) Sales and Coupons

Chapter Nineteen
Food

1) Recipes

2) Restaurant Takeout Menus

3) "Grab and Go" Snacks

4) Cook in Bulk and Freeze to Save Time and Effort

5) Remember to Take Your Dinner Out of the Freezer the Night Before

6) Keep Your Food Fresh

Chapter Twenty
Projects

1) Organizing Project Parts and Information

2) Grab and Go Fix-It Bag

Chapter Twenty-One
Organizing Specific Items

1) Medications

2) Keys

3) Pet Toys

4) Creative Storage for Kitchen Utensils

5) Paint, Paint Supplies, and Paint Samples

6) Extra Parts

7) Gift Bags and Wrapping

8) Ten Ways to Organize Those Smallest of Items

9) Cosmetics, Nail Accessories, and Hair Accessories

10) Hobby Rooms

11) Pictures

12) Movies, DVDs, Music, and CDs

13) Taming Your Cords and Wires

14) Replace That Rolodex

15) Selling Your Home

16) Garage

Chapter Twenty-Two
Recycle and Reuse

1) Recycle Those Unused Containers

2) Storage Containers

3) Baskets

4) Binders

5) What Can You Recycle?

Chapter Twenty-Three
Organizing Challenges

1) The One Week Challenge

2) Challenges to Do

Conclusion

Introduction

When most people think of organization they imagine cleaning up their home and clearing out clutter, but organization is also about family, finances, time management, stress control, and so much more. It affects every aspect of our lives and our family members' lives as well. Organization is the foundation for a successful, stress free, clutter free, happy, and fulfilling life.

If you are reading this book perhaps you have already decided you have some areas of your life or home that need to be organized.

In this book you will find a vast collection of organizing tips, short articles, and many examples to help get you started. Also included are many organizing challenges to help with any specific areas that may need attention. It's up to YOU to choose which challenges to accept and accomplish.

Each challenge has references which will lead you to the help you may need to complete each one. Try to do as many as you can (maybe schedule one a day or one every week) and add in some of your own as well.

When you are done, make sure to take the time to enjoy the rewards of being organized. You will soon be asking yourself, "Why did I wait so long?"

Happy Organizing, Everyone!

Chapter One

Why Organize?

Are you an organized person?
Is your family life more chaotic than it should be?
Does any of this describe you?

1) Stressed.

2) Low on cash.

3) Hectic schedule.

4) Low on time.

5) Low on energy.

6) Late for appointments.

7) Forget to bring essential items with you.

8) Forget to do important tasks.

9) Always looking for a lost item such as your car keys or cell phone.

10) Your house has piles of clutter you just don't have time to deal with.

11) You are running out of space in your home.

12) Your kids are constantly forgetting their homework and are not acting responsibly.

Disorganization can be stressful, time consuming, messy, and expensive!

Organization can help you and your family in many different ways:

1) Reduces clutter, helping to maximize your space so you can enjoy more of your home.

2) Saves money and improves overall finances by helping you take full advantage of savings and opportunities available to you. No more late payments from bills that were forgotten and not paid on time. No more loss of savings such as tax deductions, insurance claims, rebates, and coupons because the paperwork was lost. No more increased repair costs caused by forgotten maintenance. No more missed opportunities to advance in your career caused by lack of organization and preparation.

3) Saves time for you and your family. No more wasted time looking for lost items, making you late for appointments or special events. No more wasted time running back and forth to the store, purchasing items you didn't know you already had. No more multiple trips for multiple items.

2

4) Reduces stress for a healthy lifestyle by simplifying daily activities and improving everyday life. No more forgotten items when leaving home. No more schedule conflicts and arguments caused by lack of communication. No more forgotten homework and responsibilities from the kids.

5) Improves your quality of life with all the above.

Chapter Two

Some Things to Keep in Mind While Organizing

One thing to keep in mind—and you will notice this stated many times throughout this book—is to start by tossing everything you no longer want or need and categorize the rest. These are extremely important steps that will help you save space, control clutter, and quickly find what you need.

There are many other things everyone should keep in mind while organizing. Here are a few of those things:

The ABC's of Organization

A place for everything and everything in its place.

Be prepared and bring a Busy Bag with you to get things done while you wait.

Categorize your items before storing them away.

Different ways to organize. There is more than one way to organize. Choose the way that works best for you and your family.

*E*veryone shares household responsibilities.

*F*amily budget. Create one and stick to it.

*G*et rid of clutter, file those piles of papers, clear out that junk drawer, and organize that pantry.

*H*elp each other organize and come up with more ideas.

*I*nformation is important. Create a family communication area with a family calendar and post all necessary information.

*J*oy: it's what you will feel when you're done organizing. You will also feel a real sense of accomplishment and reduced stress knowing you are now organized.

*K*ids need to be organized too!

*L*earn how to live an organized, stress free, clutter-free life, and maintain that organization.

*M*iscellaneous. Avoid labeling any files, drawers, or storage boxes "Miscellaneous."

*N*o is a powerful word. Use it when you need more time for yourself and your family and don't want to become overwhelmed.

*O*rganize now to save time and money and reduce stress and clutter.

*P*rocrastination: fight it!

*Q*uickly put away a few items at a time: five minutes, five items.

*R*educe stress. Plan ahead, stock up on everyday items, leave a few minutes early, etc.

*S*ee it, find it. Store your items in clear containers to see it and find it quickly.

*T*o do lists. Have one going at all times so you can quickly decide what to do with those extra few minutes in the day.

*U*nused and unwanted items need to go. Hold a garage sale, recycle and throw things away, or donate to your favorite charity.

*V*ertically store your items to save storage space.

*W*rite it down. Don't rely on your memory for everything, write reminder notes.

X marks the spot. Mark the spot where you planted seeds in the garden and are now expecting them to grow, mark a spot in the garage with a hanging tennis ball or soft cone to know where to stop the car so you don't bump into anything important, mark the spot where the end of the driveway is with reflective markers so when the snow covers everything you will still know where the end of the driveway is, etc.

Organize Your Life and More ~ Christina Scalise

Yes. Say yes to those who offer to help you.

Zzzzzz. Take a break, take a nap, take time for yourself, and enjoy how organized you have become.

Realistic Organization

Nothing will ever be 100% organized 100% of the time. Do not stress over having everything perfect. Organization isn't about perfection; it's about efficiency, reducing stress and clutter, saving time and money, and improving your quality of life.

Sometimes Less Really Is More

The less you keep, the easier it will be to find the more important items. So get rid of as many items as you can that you no longer want or need. Donate, sell, or toss, it's up to you. Once you have cleaned out the items you no longer want or need, you will notice a wonderful feeling of relaxation and liberation!

A Place for Everything and Everything in Its Place

How many times have you heard this expression? It really is very good advice. Each week, take the time to look around your home at the items that are still sitting out; odds are that a lot of these items do not have a designated place in your home. Once you have designated a place for each item, you will suddenly find it easier to keep your items put away and your home will become clutter-free in no time. So make a file for those unfiled papers, choose a container to store those loose items, and get rid of the items you do not need or want. And always remember to have: A place for everything and everything in its place.

Don't Try to Do it All at Once

Don't let yourself become overwhelmed with all the things that need to be organized. Make a list, prioritize, and then work on one thing at a time.

Trying to get everything organized all in one day can be extremely frustrating and often disappointing when it can't be accomplished. Instead, work on one project at a time and if you accomplish all of your goals—great! If not, simply continue moving on to the next project the following day.

Sometimes starting out with the smaller projects first will give you enough confidence and motivation to continue to the larger ones. Remember to pace yourself; do one at a time and you will be surprised at how fast they all get done and how much you will accomplish.

Different Ways to Organize

When organizing your home and family, keep in mind what works for one family may not work as well for another family. Every home, person, and family is different, and finding the best way to organize each one can sometimes be a challenge. The trick is to find what works best for you and your family and stick with it.

Using Spreadsheets to Organize Your Information

Spreadsheet programs such as Microsoft Excel let you organize your information in many different ways. I cannot stress enough that everyone should take the time to learn how to use one of these programs. They can be extremely beneficial in organizing many different things: shopping lists, family budgets, business expenses and profits, kids' chores and rules sheets, garden planting, passwords, and so much more. Organize your information in this fashion and you will be able to find the information you need quickly and easily.

Sometimes You Need to Make a Bigger Mess to Achieve Less Mess

Some organizing projects may seem unmanageable because the mess that has been created appears to be out of control. Every so often it may be necessary to take everything out and see just what you are dealing with. Then you will be able to figure out how you want to tackle that organizing project.

Start by taking everything out of that area, drawer, or shelf and lay it all out on a flat surface where you can easily see everything.

Next, go through the items one by one and separate them into two different categories: items you are keeping, and items you are not keeping. Immediately discard the items you are not keeping.

Last, organize what you are keeping into separate categories. If necessary, place them into subcategories as well. Then place them back on the shelf, in the drawer, or in the cabinet.

For example, if you are organizing a pantry:

Category 1*: Canned items*

    Subcategories: corn, peas, beans, beets, etc.

Category 2: Cereals

Category 3: Snack items

> *Subcategories: crackers, chips, popcorn, etc.*

Category 4: Condiments

> *Subcategories: ketchup, mustard, relish, salad dressings, steak sauce, etc.*

Category 5: Paper products

> *Subcategories: paper towels, napkins, paper plates, etc.*

Category 6: Dinner and side dish items

> *Subcategories: pastas, rice, stuffing, potatoes, etc.*

Category 7: Baking and cooking ingredients

> *Subcategories: cake mixes, flour, sugar, bread crumbs, spices, etc.*

Category 8: Peanut butter and jelly

Category 9: Drinks

> *Subcategories: soda, juice, water, sports drinks, etc.*

Category 10: Food wraps

> *Subcategories: plastic wrap, foil, wax paper, freezer bags, etc.*

Group your items together by placing one in front of the other, one on top of the other, or put them together in containers. The purpose of grouping your items together before you put them away is so you can quickly see what you have without having to search for any particular item.

Make it Work for You

The main reason for organization is to make life easier and less stressful. Sometimes you put so much effort into organizing and setting up a system for yourself, you can't see that what you have done may not work best for your lifestyle.

If you organized an area and it is not working out as well as you had hoped, you may have to consider reorganizing, or at the very least adjusting a few things to make it work.

Sometimes putting in that little bit of extra effort can make all the difference.

Family Members

They do not always cooperate with new organizing methods. Make sure to find a way that works best for *your family,* then make sure everyone knows how the new system works and give them plenty of time to adjust.

Keep in mind that it often takes up to a month to learn a new way of doing things and make it part of the normal routine.

Maintenance is the key to *staying* organized. If family members still aren't cooperating with the new organizing system, it may be time to ask their opinion on how they would like to make changes or adjustments to help make it work for them.

Keep the lines of communication open and be sure to explain the benefits of any new organizing system. Once everyone in the family agrees on the new system, cooperation should no longer be a problem.

Labels

A helpful new habit for all family members to learn is to make sure when you place a box, container, or any other labeled item away, always make sure the label is showing.

Whether it's a label you have created or a manufacturer's label, searching for any item is a lot quicker and easier when the labels are facing forward where you can see them.

Success=Organization

&

Organization=Success

Think about it—have you ever seen anyone who was successful and NOT organized? Most successful people are either organized, or at the very least have an organized person running things for them. Organization is the key to success.

Chapter Three

Finding Ambition and Avoiding Interruptions

Finding the ambition to keep you going, the help you need, and the time to accomplish all of your goals can be a challenge. And messy family members can often make this even more discouraging.

Here are a few things to help keep you going:

Remember Why

Remembering why you wanted to get organized in the first place can be just enough to keep you going.

Here are a few things to help keep you motivated to organize and get the job done. You may want to:

1) Make room for a new purchase.

2) Redecorate.

3) Save money.

4) Save time, having more time for the fun stuff.

5) Reduce stress and enjoy life more.

6) Reduce clutter and maximize space in your home.

7) Remember the important things.

8) Have the ability to find your keys every day without going on a hunt.

Play some music to keep your mood upbeat and invite some helpers (you can offer to help them get organized in exchange) and start organizing!

Focus on Areas of the Greatest Concern

When choosing what to organize first, keep your focus on areas concerning you the most and that will change your life for the better. For instance:

1) If your bills are being paid late, work on creating a family budget and set up a bill-paying system so you will not forget to pay them on time.

2) If you are continuously forgetting to grab your cell phone before leaving the house, create an area to store your cell phone by your car keys, or leave a permanent reminder note by your keys reminding you to grab your cell phone before you leave.

3) If you constantly forget to put the garbage out on garbage day, take the time to write down a reminder on your calendar on each day it needs to go out, or simply place a reminder card in a place you will be sure to see.

4) If your kids aren't doing their chores, type up a chore sheet and have the rules clearly written down on paper. They can easily see what they can and cannot have if

their chores are done or not done. And always make sure to follow through on the rules.

5) If you start organizing in areas that need it the most, you will immediately feel the difference and be more motivated to move on to the next organizing project.

Make Cleaning and Organizing Fun

Cleaning and organizing can seem like a never-ending job, but if you try to make it fun it can be a truly positive experience. Here are a few things you can try, to help make it fun:

1) Play upbeat music.

2) Invite friends and family who are fun to work with, and offer to help them organize in return.

3) Give yourself a reward for finishing each task.

4) Think of all the calories you are burning moving around while cleaning up. What a great way to get some exercise!

5) For kids:

    a) Make it a race to see who can finish first, or if they finish within a certain time frame, offer a reward.

    b) Play a game of basketball by keeping a toss bin handy with a strict rule that only non-breakable items may be tossed into it.

c) Make a dust puppet out of an old sock and tell them to have the puppet help them clean the dust.

Remember to try to make it as fun and enjoyable as possible and you will be done in no time.

January is National Organizing Month

Why not start out the New Year with some organization? What a great way to start the New Year! Make it a New Year's resolution to get organized as much as possible in your life. Begin each month with a new goal or organizing challenge.

Fighting Procrastination

Procrastination can keep you from doing so many different things around your home. Sometimes you just cannot figure out where to begin. Lack of cooperation and help from family members can also diminish your motivation to even get started. Insist that everyone do their part and then choose an area of your home and push yourself to get started on it. Don't insist that it all has to be done in one day, and don't expect perfection. Instead, focus on making things better for you and your family and take on one project at a time, making sure to set aside enough time each day to do each one. Work on one project, one room, one drawer, one box, or one area at a time and give yourself plenty of time for each task and unexpected interruptions.

Examples: Every night, pull out one box that has been in storage and go through it while watching television, or clean out the pantry, refrigerator, or junk drawer.

Taking on too much at one time can be very frustrating and slow you down tremendously. Choose one task or project daily and stick to it until you have accomplished everything you would like done.

Learn to Say No

Today everyone seems to have a very hectic schedule and there never seems to be enough time for the important things in life anymore. Sometimes saying the word "no" can be a hard thing to do, but it's very important in reducing everyday stress. Part of being organized is being able to keep up with daily life, reducing the stress and still having enough time for family and the fun stuff, too. When you commit to too many things and take on more than you can handle, it can be very stressful and very time consuming. It is then time to ask yourself, "Is it really worth being committed to so many different things?"

Next time you are asked to add something to your schedule, ask yourself if it is truly worth your time to try and fit it in. If it's not, try saying a very polite "no thank you," or at the very least ask if someone else can help share the task at hand. Set up a family schedule, including the kids, to share the household chores, and when volunteering, ask that everyone do their part to help out.

Some people also reserve one day a week for family time and use that as a general rule to help them politely turn down invitations and requests. Taking one day to relax and recuperate from the week's activities is a great way to get in quality time with your family and help reduce stress.

The "To Do" List

Organize Your Life and More ~ Christina Scalise

"To Do" lists are very important. Unfortunately, for some people, trying to accomplish everything on their To Do list can seem like a never-ending battle. Right next to that list should be a "Life Goals" list.

Think of all the fun things you want to do and the goals you want to accomplish in life: take a trip, run a marathon, be debt-free by age forty, and more. Getting our life goals organized and laid out on paper is essential. Seeing them in writing reminds us what is important to each of us as individuals, and just like a To Do list, it gives us more of an incentive to get each one done and marked off.

So create a Life Goals list today and have your family members create one, too. You will be surprised at how many are similar and can be accomplished together.

And as far as the To Do list goes: start each day by prioritizing your list and take on each task one at a time. Just remember, for every so many To Dos you should probably be doing at least one Life Goal as a reward for your accomplishments. Life is too short not to enjoy it.

Pick a Number and Challenge Yourself

To help reduce clutter, challenge yourself to get rid of, donate, or sell a minimum of five (or any other number you may choose) unneeded items each week, and have other family members do the same. Go through your cabinets, closets, garage, attic, basement, bedroom, and get rid of drinking glasses, coffee cups, toys, files, clothes, shoes, books, movies, etc. Start sorting through those items that have built up over the years. You will be amazed at how easy it is to find things in your home you no longer want or need, and doing this on a regular basis will help reduce the clutter and give you much more room for storage and living space.

Five Minutes

Maintaining household organization can seem overwhelming at times, especially when the clutter is starting to get out of control. Prevention and maintenance are very important. Taking five minutes out of every day to deal with something that usually gets out of control very quickly can prevent the stressful buildup of clutter and disorganization. Schedule five minutes every day and go through ALL of the mail, file some of your paperwork, or just pick up things that were left out. If five minutes doesn't work for you, try a different amount of time: five minutes, ten minutes, or even an hour, whatever works for *you*. You will be surprised at how much you can accomplish when you schedule it in.

Avoid Interruptions to Get the Job Done

Getting anything accomplished can be difficult if you are constantly being interrupted. Help reduce interruptions using these five simple guidelines:

1) Learn to say no and do not overextend your schedule before you even get started. Make sure you have set aside enough time to start and finish every task.

2) Let everyone know you are busy for that time period and only emergency interruptions are acceptable.

3) Close the door to the room where you are working. If necessary, place a Do Not Disturb sign on the door.

4) Only allow prescheduled break times for lunch and checking email and phone messages.

5) Turn off your cell phone and let callers leave messages if necessary.

6) Shut off anything that produces a distracting noise (television, radio, computer, etc.)

With a little bit of restraint and willfulness you can get the job done on time without any interruptions.

No More Excuses

For every excuse you and your family members have used to remain unorganized, there is a solution. Here are some to consider

1) "I don't have time." (The most common excuse.)

   a) The fact remains, the more organized you are, the more time you will save.

   b) Wake up a few minutes earlier every morning (5 to 15 minutes to start) and spend that extra time doing a quick cleanup.

   c) Maintain the organization to prevent large messes from happening in the first place.

   d) See "Time" (Chapter 10) and "Plan Ahead" (Chapter 11) for more time saving tips.

2) "There's too much stuff! I don't know where to start!" Taking on too much at once can be extremely overwhelming.

   a) Start with one box, one item or one area at a time.

b) Start with a small, easy project and slowly work your way up to the harder tasks.

c) Start with the most problematic areas first to see the most impact. The positive results will give you the motivation to continue on to the next organizing project.

3) "I don't know where to put it all."

a) Take time to purge unneeded or unwanted items to create more storage room, then group like items together and place them where you will easily find them when needed.

4) "I can't afford it."

a) Recycle and reuse everyday household items to help you organize. For more information on how to recycle and reuse, see the following chapters:

   I. Keep It Stored Vertically (Chapter 6).

   II. Springtime Planting (Chapter 17).

   III. Ten Ways to Organize Those Smallest of Items (Chapter 21).

   IV. Recycle and Reuse (Chapter 22).

5) "I can't get rid of it, someone gave it to me."

a) Simply put: If you don't use it or enjoy it; donate, sell, or toss the item or give it to someone who will enjoy it.

6) "I can't do it all by myself."

a) Get help from others. See Getting Help (Chapter 4) for more information.

7) "It won't stay organized."

   a) Explain the new organizing system to all family members. Ask if there are any questions or suggestions for improvement, and then create chore and rules sheets, if necessary, for family members to follow.

   b) Show by example that it can be and should be done.

   c) Make it a habit to take that extra step to pick up after yourself immediately; do not leave anything out to deal with later.

8) "No one will throw anything out."

   a) Encourage family members to donate their unwanted and unneeded items to local charities.

   b) Let your family members know just how good it feels to lift the burden of clutter.

   c) Show your newly organized areas to demonstrate just how nice an organized area can look and feel.

   d) Let them know you won't be offended if they throw out, sell, or donate something you have given them in the past.

   e) Negotiate. Example: You throw out one item they don't like, and they throw out one item you don't like.

9) "I don't know how."

   a) Find the help you need:

      I. Read the rest of this book.

      II. Research tips online.

      III. Ask friends how they've done it.

10) "I can't pass up a bargain."

    a) Avoid the shopping areas where you bring home the most unusable and unneeded items.

    b) Ask yourself these questions:

        I. Where will I store it?

        II. Will it fit in my home?

        III. Will it be useful?

        IV. Do I really need it?

        V. Do I really need that many?

11) "It's a waste of money to throw it away."

    a) It's also a waste of money, time, effort, space, and stress storing the unneeded or unwanted item in your home. If you cannot sell the item, simply donate or toss it.

12) "I don't know how long I have to keep this piece of paper."

    a) Follow the guidelines listed under: What and When to Toss (Chapter 13).

13) "I don't know what to keep and what to get rid of."

    a) Ask yourself these questions:

        I. Do I need it?

        II. Do I love it?

        III. Is it useful?

        IV. Can I sell it?

     V. Can I donate it?

    VI. Can I recycle it?

   VII. Can someone else use or enjoy it?

  VIII. Have I used it in the past year?

    IX. How many do I need?

14) "I can't keep up with the mess."

   a) Spend five minutes a day going through clutter.

   b) Put things away immediately.

   c) Go through the mail as soon as it comes in.

   d) For every item you bring into your home, throw out one item.

   e) Schedule time (a few minutes will do) to pick up every day.

15) "I might need it one day."

   a) If you haven't used it within the past year, you most likely never will.

   b) If you have more than one, ask yourself: How many do I really need to keep?

Chapter Four

Getting Help

Sometimes the best way to get organized is to get help from a friend. Someone who can help you tackle the problem by looking at it from a different perspective. Choose a weekend and spend one day at your home and one day at your friend's home. Friends can help each other stay focused and motivated to finish the task at hand.

Help Wanted

Need help with household chores? Have family members who have extra time on their hands? Have you ever thought of posting a "Help Wanted" sign in your home? It may sound like a silly idea, but it works great for busy parents with children who need to earn some extra cash, work off punishments, or who may just want to earn extra privileges. Having available jobs already listed can be very useful. This list should be posted in an area where everyone in the family will see it. List jobs by age requirement, or simply create a separate list for each child.

Be creative, make it fun, and make sure to add in rules that go along with the available jobs you have listed, such as:

1) All pay rates (or benefits) will be based on job performance.

2) Trading one of your chores for a job that is listed is acceptable if approved by Mom or Dad.

3) Doing one of these jobs may entitle you to extra privileges.

4) Smiling and working with a positive attitude is optional and may help you earn a little more.

If necessary, consider posting the benefits of each job listed such as pay, extra privileges earned, etc. Try posting available jobs in different ways until you find a way that works best for your family.

Posting Help Wanted signs can be beneficial to everyone in the family if you make it worth everyone's time and effort.

How to Get Your Kids to Help With Household Chores

Getting your children to help out with household chores can be a challenge, but it is very important to help them develop self-confidence, a sense of pride, responsibility, and a good work ethic. It can also be a great way for them to earn a bit of cash or extra privileges while doing their part to help with household chores. Here are a few things to take into consideration when trying to get that extra bit of help you need from everyone, including the kids.

1) Start at an early age and make sure everyone in the family participates. Have chores written down clearly on individual or family chore charts so it is clear what needs to be done and when.

2) Make sure you are giving each child chores that are age appropriate and safe for them to do.

3) Give them several chores to choose from and let them choose which ones they will be responsible for.

4) Have everyone take turns doing different chores or allow family members to trade chores with other family members. This helps keep things fair for everyone and prevents boredom.

5) Everyone needs a day off every now and then; once a week, on the weekends, or on birthdays. Give each person a specific day off to rest, or choose a certain number of days to take off per week or per month. When a child is overwhelmed by the day's activities, homework, and more, it can also help to let them take an additional day off on that day as well. Just try to limit how many times it is allowed per week or month to avoid abuse of that privilege.

6) For older children, have them create their own recipe books and they can soon start helping with the cooking as well. You can use a regular binder with page protectors or photo insert pages to hold recipes. Have

them decorate the cover and start them off with a few of their favorite recipes that you would usually cook for them.

7) Be positive and give incentives or rewards such as cash or special privileges. Make sure to communicate that not every chore will be rewarded; some are just them doing their part. If they would like to earn extra cash you can create an extra jobs list that gives everyone a chance to earn extra cash or even additional privileges by doing work voluntarily.

Children can greatly benefit from contributing to the family work load; it can be very rewarding in many different ways, and can also be a lot of fun.

How to Get Help Doing the Laundry

Doing the laundry, even separating the laundry prior to washing it, can be very time consuming. For those of us who have larger families, keeping up with the constant flow of laundry can be overwhelming at times. If you cannot get everyone in the family to take turns doing the laundry or have each of them do their own laundry, consider the following:

Laundry rooms need organization too. If you have enough room in your laundry room, set up different laundry baskets or bins for different colors (whites, darks, and colors), special care, and rinse-first items. Next, label these baskets and bins so EVERYONE in the family will know where to place each item.

28

For parents who do a lot of laundry: How many times have you seen a dirty, mud-covered sock all bunched up and inside out and thought to yourself: I do not want to put my hand inside of that! If kids can't be responsible enough to have their clothes properly prepared for the laundry basket, try setting up a rejected bin as well, and place any clothes that were not properly prepared into this bin. Have a list of reasons why clothes would end up in this bin posted right next to it, such as: clothes that have items still in the pockets, clothes that are inside out or bunched up, or even clothes that are not placed into the proper laundry basket. After you have rejected a certain amount of clothing, your children will soon decide it is worth it to do what needs to be done the first time and you should no longer need a rejected bin. Just make sure everyone in the family is aware of the rejected bin ahead of time, what the rules are, and what they will need to do to avoid having their clothes end up there.

Have a designated area in your laundry room (on a shelf or in cubbies), right next to your washer and dryer, for each person's clothing to be placed until they are ready to be put away. Then have each family member be responsible for putting away their own pile of laundry each day. This area can also be used for separating the mail and anything else that was not previously put away by each member of the family. If you do not have time or just don't want to bother folding smaller items such as socks, have a Clean Bin available to place them in and have everyone grab what is theirs out of the bin each time they pick up their pile of clothes.

Organize Your Life and More ~ Christina Scalise

If everyone in the family does their part to pitch in, laundry will become an easier chore to keep up with and everyone will benefit with clean clothes and less stress.

If You Want Something Done, Ask a Busy Person to Do It

Unfortunately for the busy people, this commonly used phrase is very true. Most busy people know how to avoid wasting time and usually get the job done without procrastinating.

If you need help getting organized, ask a busy person for help, or just ask them for some inspiration. Maybe they could think of some ideas to help get you started.

Chapter Five

Organizing Products

If You Choose to Purchase New Organizing Products, visit *OrganizeYourLifeAndMore.com* for more information, tips, products, and product recommendations.

Here are some other places where you can find more organizing products:

1) Local Stores:

   a) General store.

   b) Office supply store.

   c) Home improvement store.

   d) Dollar store.

2) Search the Internet for:

   a) Organizing products.

   b) Office supplies.

   c) Home improvement stores.

   d) Containers.

31

Label Makers

Label makers are admittedly one of my favorite toys and are great tools for neat and quick labeling. They are very useful in helping you quickly label file folders, binders, envelopes, storage containers, boxes, shelves, drawers, plant pots, and so much more.

Labeling items around your home can save you time and money. How many times have you purchased an item just to discover you had already purchased that same item and either completely forgot about it or just could not find it? How many times have you lost valuable paperwork just to find it later when it was no longer useful? How many times have you overlooked a file you were looking for just because the label on it didn't stand out enough for you to notice? Clearly labeled files and containers are much easier to identify with typed labels because the neatly written label stands out much more than handwritten labels do, saving you precious searching time. Invest in a good label maker and it will pay for itself in no time.

DYMO produces many easy-to-use label makers and also sells different sizes of labels for many diverse uses, even postage labels for mailing. You can find these label makers and many others just like them available online or at your local office supply store.

Clear Containers Are Best For Storing Items Away

If you don't want to label a lot of your storage containers try using clear containers. You will know just what is inside with one quick look and are less likely to have to label it. If you don't have clear containers available, try using different colors that you would associate with the items stored inside. Examples: Red or Green: Christmas items. Black or Orange: Halloween items. Child's favorite color: child's favorite items.

Square vs. Round

Choosing the correct storage container can help you save space in areas where you need it the most. If you have ever tried to fit several large, round food containers in the refrigerator at one time, you know just what I am talking about. Food storage containers are one of those items that often come in round shapes. When shopping for any type of storage containers, look for those that are square or rectangular in shape. Using round ones will always waste space when stacked next to each other. Square and rectangular shaped containers fit neatly together and will help you maximize your space.

Adjustable Shelving

The one thing you can count on in life is constant change. Adjusting to life's changes isn't always easy, but adjusting your surroundings should be. When purchasing any type of shelving, look for those that are adjustable. Adjustable shelving is a great idea for almost any area in your home: in the closet, kitchen, pantry, office, garage, cellar, and bedrooms. Adjustable shelving will help fit your changing storage needs.

Chapter Six

How to Store Your Items

Try not to label files or boxes "Miscellaneous." Items can easily be lost or forgotten this way. Instead, designate a place for as many items as possible. And mark each file, box, or container with the contents inside.

If you have a drawer filled with miscellaneous items or papers mixed up in what you would describe as a miscellaneous filing system, try separating them into as many categories as possible.

See Chapter 8 for more information on How to Organize a Junk Drawer.

Categorize Before You Organize

Make sure you separate items into categories before storing them away. Putting items away quickly in a random manner will cause an unneeded search when trying to find things later on. You also will not have the advantage of quickly knowing exactly what you have in stock and what you will need the next time you go shopping.

Sometimes the best way to clean up a huge, unorganized mess is to just lay it all out, separate into categories, and then store it away.

Keep It Stored Vertically

When storing items such as storage container lids, baking pans, paper plates, notepads, pens, pencils, markers, binders, file folders, books, and envelopes, store them in an upright position instead of stacking them one on top of the other. This not only saves space, but also makes it easier for you to quickly grab each item.

You can purchase vertical dividers for your kitchen items; for smaller items such as pens, pencils, and markers, you can use pencil and pen organizers (available at most office supply stores). Or you can recycle and use any large plastic cup, thick vase, or clear plastic container (containers for deli olives and take-out food work great). If you use a container that is clear or at least clear enough to see the items inside, it will make it a lot easier to find each item you are looking for.

Stack and Store Vertically or Horizontally to Save Room

Many items can be stored one on top of the other for easy access both vertically and horizontally, including many boxed items. Either way (horizontally or vertically), it saves room.

Organize Your Life and More ~ Christina Scalise

Here are a few items to consider stacking either way to save room in your cabinets.

1) Boxed items:

    a) Cereals.

    b) Pastas.

    c) Soups.

2) Paper products:

    a)   Paper towels.

    b)   Toilet paper rolls.

    c)   Tissues.

    d)   Paper plates and cups.

If you have several different varieties of the same type of product, be sure to group the different varieties together. This way you can easily see what you have on hand and quickly choose which one you will need at the time.

Make it Stand Out with Colors

For storage containers, notes, lists, calendars, and filing systems, try using different colors to make those important items stand out.

With storage containers, baskets, and boxes use different colored containers, baskets, or boxes. If you would like all of them to match, use different colored labels instead. In time, when you are looking for each one, you will find yourself looking for the right color before you even start reading labels.

On your calendar, mark each repetitive reminder in one bright color so you will notice it right away. Use different colors for different family members or each type of event or appointment.

When you leave yourself a note, use brightly colored paper. Post-its now come in many different colors and this helps each one stand out. Brightly colored index cards can also be used for making notes.

When creating lists, whether it is a grocery list or a To Do list, highlight the important items with a bright color.

For your filing system, use different color tabs or different color files to make the most used or most important files stand out from the rest.

Alphabetize or Sort By Size and Color

There are many ways to organize your items. When you have a lot of the same type of items, sometimes it is best to sort things alphabetically or by size and color. Alphabetizing is a great way to organize your files, paperwork, books, spices, and more. For other items such as small tools and hardware items like nails, screws, nuts, and bolts, sorting them by size may be the better solution. With clothes, crafts, colored paper, and paints, try sorting by color. Use the organizing solution that works best for you.

Save the Small Stuff

Saving every item that has sentimental value can lead to a cluttered home in no time. Try to limit what you save to items that can be easily stored without overwhelming your home. Get creative and try to save space. Example: Instead of saving large school projects that your children have worked on, try taking a picture of the child holding the project and save the picture instead.

What to Store in Fireproof Containers or Safety Deposit Box

1) Jewelry.

2) Vehicle titles.

3) Stocks.

4) Birth certificates.

5) Marriage license.

6) Property deeds and titles.

7) Will.

8) Passport.

9) Social security card.

10) Insurance policies (home, life, etc.).

11) Photos.

12) Personal records such as:

    a) Personal banking information.

    b) Credit card numbers.

    c) Pin numbers.

    d) Passwords.

    e) Combinations.

Also consider creating a backup file on your hard drive which should include scans of all of the above items. This, or a copy of this file, should be kept in another location.

Empty Containers and Lids

One thing most households have plenty of is containers. Before organizing them, go through each container and make sure they all have matching lids and make sure each lid has a matching container. If not, then simply toss or recycle.

Once you have tossed the ones you no longer want to keep, separate the rest by shape so you can easily stack one inside the other. And make sure to place all covers in an area close to their matching containers.

Stacking the lids with the containers can be messy if there are a lot of them. If there are too many lids and they are starting to fall over and make a mess, consider placing them vertically in a cupboard or in a separate clear container all their own, or simply purchase a lid organizer (vertical or horizontal).

If you have plenty of space and want to store each lid with its matching container, try placing several of the same types of containers together (one inside the other if possible) with the matching lids stacked on top of them to save as much room as possible. But, keep in mind this can waste more space than if you simply separate lids from containers.

Visualize to Organize; See it, Find it

Can you easily find your belongings when needed? If not, you may want to walk through your home and apply the following strategy to every item you own. This includes everything from your spice cabinet, freezer, and pantry, to items stored away in boxes in your attic, cellar, and garage. Anything that is not currently visible should be.

If something needs to be stored away, store it in clear containers so you can quickly determine what is inside, or store it in a clearly labeled container that lists all contents stored inside. Always remember to visualize when you organize; if you can see it, you will find it.

Pegboards

Holding tools in the garage is not the only place and purpose for a pegboard. Hang them in places you normally wouldn't, such as:

1) In the office to hang supplies.

2) In the closet to hang purses, belts, jewelry, and small mirrors.

3) In the bedroom to hang a calendar, jewelry, and hair accessories.

4) In the kitchen to hold utensils, pots, and pans.

5) In the laundry room or mudroom to hold brooms, dustpans, ironing board, and supplies.

They can also hold small shelves, clocks, décor, and so much more. Pegboards are a great way to organize so many things and can also be quite decorative.

Several ways you can decorate your pegboard:

1) Frame it.

2) Hang décor.

3) Paint a picture on it.

4) Shape it into an appealing design.

Chapter Seven

Where to Store Your Items

Creative Storage

Some unusual places to store items include: shelving underneath stairs, hanging items in between rafters, and placing a few hooks along the wall inside a closet or cabinet (Command Brand strips and clips are great for this because they are easily removable and do no damage).

To eliminate wasted space inside your cabinets and on shelves, try placing your items vertically, or hang items underneath shelves where there is extra space.

When purchasing furniture, consider pieces that offer hidden storage. Underneath furniture (beds and couches) is also a great place to store items.

Wasted Spaces

Look at any storage areas in your home. Do you see any open spaces? If you can see the wall or floor in between stored items, you are losing valuable storage space. To use and fill in these wasted areas, adjust shelving, stack items vertically, hang items, and use small shelves on top of other shelves to elevate areas. Find any way you can to use that valuable space.

Hidden Storage Hiding in Your Cabinets

Hanging items in and underneath your cabinets can be a great way to save space.

Hang items inside your kitchen cabinets, underneath your shelves, on the door, or underneath the outside of your cabinets.

A few items you can do this with:

1) On the door, inside the cabinet:

   a) Information.

   b) Towels.

   c) Bag holders.

2) Underneath the inside or outside portion of the cabinet:

   a) Coffee cups.

   b) Wine glasses.

   c) Wine bottles.

3) Underneath the outside (bottom) of the cabinet:

   a) Bananas.

   b) Small appliances (such as a toaster oven or microwave).

Check every cabinet you have and you are sure to find some wasted space that can be utilized.

Store Away for Future Use

Prioritize your living space by immediately getting rid of what you no longer want or need, then store away the rest for future use such as:

1) Clothing you are saving for a younger child that they haven't grown into yet.

2) Items you will soon be selling or donating.

3) Older files that cannot yet be destroyed.

4) Collections that are not currently being displayed.

5) Sentimental items.

6) Seasonal items such as:

   a) Décor.

   b) Clothing.

   c) Toys.

   d) Gardening supplies.

   e) Fishing equipment.

   f) Camping equipment.

   g) Outdoor equipment.

Remember to label every storage box you pack away so you will be able to quickly and easily find what you need when you need it. The more you store away, the more living space you will have to enjoy in your home.

Within Reach

Proper placement of household items and important papers can work as a real time saver. Try storing as much as possible within reach of the area where it will be needed most.

Examples:

1) Drinking glasses: next to the refrigerator.

2) Grocery list: in the kitchen.

3) Unpaid bills: next to the area where you will be working on them.

4) Medication information: stored with the medication.

5) Stain remedies list: posted in your laundry room.

6) Emergency numbers: posted next to your home phone and stored in all cell phones.

Store Regularly Used Items Within Reach of Children

Children and smaller adults need to be able to easily reach the items they use most often. In cupboards, drawers, shelves, laundry rooms, kitchens, and pantries, all items (food, supplies, etc.) should be stored at a height that is within reach of the person who will be using that item. Trying to get to something that is out of reach can be time-consuming and stressful for everyone.

Children love their independence, and supplying them with their own drawer, cubby, or shelf to decorate, organize, and use for their items will help contribute to their independence and self-confidence. It also gives parents a better chance of having the child return their items to the proper place when they are done using them. Provide them with a drawer in the kitchen, a shelf in the cupboard, or any area they can call their own, and move other items they use to a lower shelf. Store regularly used items within reach and you will save time, reduce stress, and create independence.

Chapter Eight

Clutter Control

Did you ever notice that when certain areas of your home are cluttered and unorganized, you tend to feel more stressed and out of control, and once you have cleared out and organized that area of your home you suddenly feel a great deal of accomplishment and a lot more relaxed?

Clutter and disorganization can affect our lives in many different ways. Our minds will start to feel as cluttered as our homes, and our homes will become as cluttered as our minds.

Sometimes the best thing we can do for ourselves is take a few minutes each day to relax and clear our minds. If your schedule is jam-packed, it may be time to reprioritize and schedule in some time for yourself. Achieving peace of mind can help you think more clearly and become much more productive in less time.

Here are just a few examples of things you can do to help clear your mind:

1) Take time to sit in a quiet area for five minutes (inside or outside) without any noise around you to disturb your thoughts, and just relax.

2) Take a walk and enjoy nature.

3) Exercise.

4) Try meditation or yoga.

5) Take a long hot bath or shower.

6) When you are feeling chaotic, immediately stop what you are doing and take a few minutes to take a few deep breaths.

Find a way that works best for you and continue to clear your mind as often as necessary.

Once the clutter has been erased from your mind, you will be able to tackle the clutter in your life and in your home. Once the clutter has been banished from your life and your home, your thoughts will be clearer, your stress level will decrease, things will run much smoother, and life in general will suddenly become much easier to deal with.

General Rules to Controlling Clutter Before it Starts

Controlling clutter can sometimes be difficult, so try following these general rules:

Keep only certain things out, such as reminders (including To Do lists) and other items currently being used. All other items should be put away.

Give yourself a time frame for having to use something that is out. Example: If you haven't used a certain item within a week, put it away. Avoid saving it for later.

Think about that next purchase and avoid places where you usually end up bringing home things you really don't need. Shop with care and ask yourself these questions before making that next purchase: Where will I store it? Will it fit in my home? Will it be useful? Do I really need it? Do I really need that many?

Do a little bit every day and deal with items such as incoming mail immediately. A few minutes every day can go a long way when trying to maintain a clutter-free home.

Paperwork, magazines, and emails can also add up quickly. To prevent them from piling up, try these tips:

1) For paperwork, categorize and file away what you want to keep and immediately toss the rest. If you do not want to file some of your papers, categorize them and use desk organizers, cubbies, shelves, or drawers to store them where you will be sure to find them easily. Store as much as you can on your computer in categorized files, making sure to back up your files. Remember, the more you print, the more papers you will need to sort through later on.

2) For magazines, if you don't have time to read those magazines, cancel the subscription. If you do have time to read them, do so, then immediately recycle or give them to someone who may enjoy them. If you want to keep an article from a magazine, tear the article out and immediately place it in a file with all

other articles or place it into a folder you can take with you to places where you will need something to read.

3) For emails, unsubscribe from email lists and categorize the rest into folders, eliminating those that are no longer needed.

Sell, donate, or toss everything you no longer need or want immediately. Gather up three large boxes or bags. Mark them "Sell," "Donate," and "Toss," then go to each room in your home filling them with items you no longer want or need.

1) For the Sell items: earn some extra cash by selling your items online, at a garage sale, or at a local consignment shop.

2) For the Donate items: donate to a local charity to help those in need and receive a tax deduction at the same time.

3) For the Toss items: all garbage should be thrown out immediately. If something is no longer usable or broken beyond repair, it's time to throw it out.

Once you get rid of the clutter, make the extra effort to keep it from piling up again and you will remain clutter-free with ease.

Temporary Clutter

Most people have clutter in some area of their home. It's that area of the home where they have temporarily placed random items they just don't know what to do with. These clutter items usually do not have a designated area set aside where they can be stored, and have been placed anywhere in the home simply because it was convenient at the time.

When you temporarily place an item somewhere in your home, you are not only creating clutter but you are also taking a chance on:

1) Not being able to remember where you placed the item when you need it the most.

2) Losing time searching for that item.

3) The possibility of purchasing the same item you didn't know you already had.

4) Causing unneeded stress.

When shopping for anything new, visualize the area where you will store the item in your home, and once purchased, make sure to place it there when it's not in use. Always try to avoid the temporary placement of any item and take the extra step to designate an area for it immediately.

I Have Too Much Stuff!

Does that phrase sound familiar? When you start to organize and clean out your home, you will probably notice you have a lot of the same items that have accumulated over the years: clothes, shoes, books, movies, children's toys, stuffed animals, containers you were saving for just the right occasion, etc., etc. Look around your home. If you have this problem, go through each item and ask yourself these questions: Do I need it? Have I used it within the last year? Do I really need this many? Once you have gone through everything, make it a rule that for each new item that is brought in, one old item will go out. One in, one out. This rule should apply to the entire family.

If you are a collector who likes to display his or her collection and just cannot part with some of your items, try displaying only part of your collection at one time, then store the rest. Every month or so, take out a few different items for display. This helps keep your collection looking fresh.

For boxes that have been in storage a long time, take each box one at a time and go through the contents. If you think you don't have enough time to go through all the boxes, schedule time by getting up a few minutes earlier, or simply go through them one at a time while you are talking on the phone or watching television.

Get Rid Of Pile

Start a Get Rid Of pile and keep it going. Choose a place in your home that is easily accessible to everyone in the family (this is important) and has plenty of room for storage, such as your basement, attic, or garage. Store your unwanted items in this area and add to this pile regularly. Separate the pile of unwanted items into different categories, such as garage sale items, church donation items, items to sell online, clothing drive items, etc.

Keep all items stored in containers (large plastic containers work best) or empty cardboard boxes (always have an empty one available). This way everything will stay clean and organized for easy access later on. Now every time you come across an item you no longer want or use, all you have to do is add it to the pile. Have your children do this regularly when they clean their rooms. Give them an empty box to fill and then add it to your Get Rid Of pile. You will be amazed at how fast this pile grows and how much clutter will be removed from your home.

Make sure to limit the size of this area, and once the pile outgrows that area make it a standing rule to get rid of those items immediately.

Discard Baskets

Just like laundry baskets, discard baskets can be very handy to have available. Anyone can use them to toss in items they no longer need or want to keep. This can include clothing that no longer fits, toys no longer being used, or any other unwanted items. These baskets can be stored in any area of the home, or you can choose to have one basket in each bedroom for easier access. The easier the access to these baskets, the quicker they will fill up. Cleaning any room is much easier when everyone clears the clutter a little at a time by consistently using a discard basket.

Make sure to empty the baskets as soon as they are full to encourage consistent refilling of unwanted items. When you empty the basket, be sure to immediately place the unwanted items in the proper storage area until you can dispose of each item.

Some people have an area in their home where they collect these unwanted items until they have enough for a garage sale, to make a trip to a local charity, or to sell the items online. The important thing to remember is to have one designated area in your home to store all unwanted items until you have time to properly dispose of each item.

How to Plan a Garage Sale

Garage sales are a great way to get rid of unnecessary clutter in your home. You will need to set aside time before the sale to advertise and set things up. You can advertise several different ways: online, in the newspaper, and with flyers and signs. Make sure you are prepared for the unexpected. Consider having some of the following items available ahead of time.

1) For displaying sale items: tables, tablecloths, sheets, blankets, and clothes racks.

2) To advertise and label items: pens, markers, poster board and paper for signs, sale stickers, scissors, and tape.

3) For customers to be able to test items or disassemble larger items: batteries, light bulbs, extension cords, and screwdrivers.

4) To combine like items together: rubber bands, paperclips, small boxes, and Ziploc bags.

5) To go with your sale items: any owner's manuals you have available.

6) For unexpected weather: clear covers, tablecloths, tarps, and tents ready to cover any sale items that will be outside which should not get wet.

7) To wrap fragile items: bags, boxes, scrap paper, and bubble wrap.

8) For conducting sales and keeping track of sale items: bags, clipboard, scrap paper, pens, calculator, fanny pack, and plenty of change. For excess cash, store a second cash box securely somewhere inside your home so you are not consistently walking around with a lot of cash on you. If you have enough room, set up an empty table for your customers to cash out and to set aside sale items they would like to purchase while they continue to shop.

9) For you: a chair and something to read between sales. Catch up on some reading you have been meaning to do, or work on something on your To Do list; basically anything you can accomplish or enjoy while waiting for customers. You can also take time in between customers to straighten up and reorganize your sale items.

Make sure sale items are clean and in working order, neatly organized by category (toys, clothes, books, household items, etc.) and priced. If an item is not working properly or is missing pieces make sure to attach a note to that item ahead of time.

To make your sale an attractive and comfortable place for potential customers to shop, consider using a fan for hot days, play a radio (not too loud and nothing inappropriate), freshen the air by using air freshener sprays, plug-ins, or other scented items, use plenty of lights to accentuate your sale items, and plug in as many electrical items as possible to show they are in working condition.

With a little hard work your garage sale will be a success and your house will be clutter-free in no time.

How to Organize a Junk Drawer

Junk drawers contain many different items and can include anything from loose change, small hardware or tools, and batteries, to random papers, pens and pencils, and small office supplies. If you find yourself digging through the junk drawer to find the item you need, you should probably spend a few minutes organizing your drawer.

Start by taking everything out of the drawer and separating the items into four different piles

1) The Garbage pile: anything that is broken or too dirty to consider keeping.

2) The Get Rid Of pile: items you may want to donate or sell.

3) The Store Elsewhere pile: for items that need to be placed elsewhere. You can put these items away in their proper spots when you are done.

4) The Junk Drawer pile: for anything that will be going back into the drawer.

Once you have these piles separated, immediately throw out the Garbage pile and set aside the Get Rid Of and Store Elsewhere piles to deal with when you are done.

The Junk Drawer pile needs to be separated into categories according to use or type of item. Once this is done, take a look at the size of each pile. This will help you determine what size and shape container you will need to store each category of items in.

There are three ways you can organize your items into a junk drawer.

1) Use several small boxes, containers or baskets (use square or rectangular containers, not round; this will help maximize drawer space). These can be found around your home or in a local store and can be very useful and decorative. They can also be easily replaced and updated to fit your changing needs for the drawer.

2) Purchase a drawer organizer and separate your items into each compartment.

3) Look around your home to see if you can possibly use any other household items you may already have handy, such as an ice cube tray, flatware organizers, etc.

Once you have chosen what to use, neatly place your items back into the drawer.

The general rule that should apply when organizing your junk drawer is that you want to be able to quickly find everything in the drawer when you open it. Remember to go through your junk drawer on a regular basis and pull out whatever needs to be placed elsewhere and throw out non-essential items. Maintaining your junk drawer is crucial to quickly finding what you need inside.

Sentimental Belongings

Emotional attachment to objects and a sense of worth are sometimes the reason for keeping items we no longer need. Try to reduce that emotional pile of belongings by keeping only a few of the items that you love the most.

If you are having trouble deciding what to keep and what to get rid of, consider the following:

1) Is the item useful?

2) Do you someday want to pass the item on to another family member? If so, why not do it now?

3) If you took a picture of the item to remember it, could you then throw it out?

4) Which ones are your absolute favorites and which ones can you part with?

5) Does the item make you happy or sad? If sad, why are you holding onto sad memories?

6) Does the item need repair? Will you ever take the time to repair it as needed?

7) If you had a fire and lost the item forever, how bad would you really feel about losing it?

8) Is the item worth a lot of money? If so, why not sell it? Items are only worth money if you actually sell them.

9) Are you happy with the item or are you keeping it to make someone else happy?

10) Could someone else benefit from receiving the item? If so, consider donating it to a local charity or any other place that may be able to use it. One example: books can be donated to a local library or school.

Having emotional attachments to items can create a stockpile of clutter in a very short period of time if you don't occasionally go through them. Just remember how good it feels to have a clutter-free home and keep that clutter-free picture in mind while going through your belongings. That should help scale things down quickly.

How Many Can You Get Rid Of?

So many different items tend to pile up in our homes on a daily basis. Several of these can easily be discarded if you just take the time to go through them every now and again.

Give yourself a challenge and see how many of these items you can discard:

1) Shoes, clothing, socks, underwear.

2) Glasses, cups, coffee mugs.

3) Music CD's, movies.

4) Hair accessories.

5) Nail polish and accessories.

6) Makeup.

7) Papers.

8) Magazines.

9) Books.

10) Stuffed animals.

11) Toys.

12) Expired medications.

13) Tools.

14) Household project items.

15) Jewelry.

16) Fishing equipment.

17) Sports equipment.

18) Hunting equipment.

19) Junk drawer items.

20) Purses.

21) Hats, scarves, gloves.

22) Pens, pencils, markers.

23) Food storage containers.

24) Décor.

25) Seasonal Décor.

26) Christmas tree ornaments.

Chapter Nine

How to Remember What You Always Forget

Are you always forgetting the same thing? Do you frequently forget to grab your cell phone, put out the garbage, feed the cat, or even do something as simple as get the hair or lint off of your coat before you leave for the day? The important thing to remember about reminders is: *if you can't see it, you are most likely to forget it.* So keep that reminder note or the item itself always visible and in a place you know you will check before leaving for the day.

One place no one ever seems to think of is right on the front door, but if you think about it, you cannot possibly go out the door without seeing that note if you place it at eye level. Another thing to keep in mind is if you use the same color or type of note to remind yourself of the same thing over and over, you won't notice it as often anymore. Try mixing it up a bit by using different color notes or ink, or maybe even different shaped notes once in a while.

Try these tips: For your cell phone, try keeping a Post-it note that reminds you to bring your cell phone with you right beside your cell phone charger. Then, whenever you are charging your phone, take that reminder note and immediately place it with other items you know you won't forget to bring with you the next day (such as your purse, wallet or coat). When you have grabbed your cell phone, put the note back next to the charger for the next time you will need it. This will save you from having to write yourself the same note over and over again.

The same concept applies for taking out the garbage, feeding the cat, and other daily duties as well. Write yourself a Post-it note and leave it on your calendar, in a basket with your car keys, or in a basket with other prewritten reminder notes. Then the day you need that reminder, take the note out and place it where you will be sure to see it. When the task has been completed, put the note back for the next time you need it. For other types of reminders, such as remembering to get the hair or lint off your coat before you leave each morning, leave the lint roller right next to your coats where you will be sure to see it every time you get your coat.

Don't Forget

Ten quick hints to help you remember something important:

1) New Year calendar preparation: When you reach the last couple of months of each calendar year, preparation for the New Year should begin. If you use a standard paper calendar, purchase a family calendar large enough to accommodate your family's schedule and any reminders. Copy any important information you will need to remember from your old calendar,

such as anniversaries, birthdays, etc. Also, add in any necessary daily, weekly, and monthly reminders.

2) Remember the items you don't want to forget by placing those items or a note reminding you of those items with something you can't possibly leave without, such as your car keys.

3) Place the item near the door you will be going out of, or hang it on the door knob, so you will be sure to see it before you leave.

4) Set a timer. This can help with many things, such as reminding you when to take your medicine or when to take a cake out of the oven.

5) In the past, people would tie a string around their finger to help them remember something. These days you can be a bit more creative by designating a certain piece of jewelry as a reminder piece, and wear it on days you need to remember something specific.

6) Have a reminder list that can be easily changed (such as an erasable board) in a place that you walk by every day, and make it part of your routine to check it at the same time every day.

7) Call and leave yourself a message on your answering machine.

8) Email yourself a reminder.

9) Use a small notebook to write yourself notes throughout the day, or use your cell phone notepad feature to type in reminder notes.

10) To remember where something important is, always be consistent and place your items in the same place day after day to avoid losing them.

Where to Write it Down

Trying to remember everything can be stressful. Writing reminder notes to yourself will help ease the stress of trying to remember the important things. The hard part is figuring out where to write and place these notes so you will see them and remember to read them.

There are several places you can try:

1) Small notebook. Always have a pen and small notebook handy to write down your reminders throughout the day.

2) Cell phone. Most cell phones now have a notepad feature where you can write yourself a note; or simply send yourself a reminder email from your cell phone.

3) Post-it note, index card, or scrap paper. If you prefer using Post-it notes, index cards, or scrap paper, make sure to keep ALL notes stored in the same place until you have had time to read them. This way you will know just where to find them when needed.

4) Computer Post-it note. Some computer programs now have digital style Post-it features called "sticky note"

that you can post directly on your computer screen. You can also download these digital notes to your computer from the Internet. Some of these programs are: "Post-it Digital Notes," "Simple Sticky Notes," "EditPad Lite," "TED Notepad," and "NoteZilla."

5) Calendar. Write your reminder notes on your calendar on the day you will need each reminder.

Create a Set of Instructions

You can avoid saying or hearing these words: "I can't remember how to do that; I will figure it out later!"

Do you or other members of your family consistently procrastinate with certain jobs around the house because you just can't remember how to do them? For those tasks you can't remember how to do and for the equipment you can't remember how to operate, write up a set of instructions and post them close to the item or work area where they are needed most.

Example:

Problem*:* Your kids never remember how to use the washing machine or which detergent to use with certain clothes.

Solution*:* Write or type a step-by-step set of instructions on how to use the washing machine properly. On the bottom of the page, list detergent types and clothing types each can be used with, then place the instructions on the inside of a cabinet door in the laundry room or post them on the wall near the washing machine.

Make sure instructions are written so everyone in the family will understand them. Doing this will help you and others in your family quickly remember how to do things correctly, so everyone can help out with household chores without the added stress of not knowing how to do it.

If you do not want instructions posted, try filing them away in a place that is easily accessible to everyone. Keep them together in one file box or drawer with each file labeled "Instructions to..." or "How to…" or simply file the instructions in the front of each file that holds the original paperwork that came with that particular item.

Keep instructions handy and you will avoid procrastination, errors, and unneeded stress.

"I Can't Remember Where I Put It!"

Searching for lost items can be very frustrating and time consuming. Wouldn't it be nice to be able to find the items you need whenever you need them? If you find yourself endlessly searching for something, consider giving that particular item a new storage place so the next time anybody needs it they will know right where to find it.

Proper placement of items isn't always easy. If one location doesn't work well, try somewhere else. Try to remember to keep like items together in an area that seems appropriate for each item, such as all outdoor items in the garage or shed, all bathroom items in the bathroom, all gardening items in the gardening shed, etc. Avoid temporary placement, and create a permanent storage area for each item. Once you have established a permanent spot you will find it is much easier to locate that item the next time you need it.

Remember to Pay Those Bills on Time!

Do you pay your bills weekly, every other week, or whenever you have time? Do you occasionally miss a due date because you forgot a bill was due? If you do not pay bills immediately upon receiving them, try this tip: as soon as you receive bills place them in a special place in your home where you will be sure to see them every day. If you have a calendar you check every day, try placing the bills right next to it so you will be sure to see them every day. You can also try marking the outside of each envelope with the due date and the amount due as soon as it comes in, then place them in order by due date, one in front of the other. Then you will know with a quick glance each day if anything needs to be paid right away.

If you receive paperless statements by email and forget to check your email regularly, write a reminder note on your calendar when each bill should be paid, or try writing it on a small sticky note and move this sticky note to the proper due date each month. Once it is paid move it to the next month's due date. This way you won't have to keep re-writing the same note over and over again.

If you would rather invest in a money management program such as Quicken or Microsoft Money, make sure to research each program's features prior to purchasing it to make sure it's the right one for you. There are many features to these programs besides reminding you when to pay your bills on time. They can also help you track your financial accounts, download transactions directly from your bank to help balance your checkbook, prepare for retirement, and much more.

Whether you decide to pay for a financial program or keep track of your finances yourself, keeping track will help you pay those bills on time, helping to eliminate late fees and overdrawn fees.

Index Card Reminders

Instead of writing yourself the same reminder note over and over again, try using brightly colored index cards. This is a great way to remember those things you are always forgetting.

You can store these cards anywhere you think you will notice them. I store a few of mine near my car keys so when I grab them I will also be reminded to grab my cell phone, bring out the garbage, set the oven timer for dinner, etc. You can also post them on the fridge, the mirror, the television; anything you find yourself looking at every day. As I have learned over the years, there are just too many things to try to remember on your own; you have to write them down.

Several reminder items you may consider placing on reusable index cards:

1) Bring out the garbage.

2) Do homework.

3) Don't forget cell phone.

These cards can also be stored with your family calendar to help remind other family members as well. You can place special events on a card made for each month of the year and place these cards next to your family calendar so you don't have to consistently write them over and over again on each year's calendar. You can do this with:

1) Birthdays.

2) Anniversaries.

3) Special events.

4) Time frames for expecting something you look forward to every year.

5) Daily or weekly scheduled events.

6) Any other monthly reminder needed.

Using brightly colored index cards helps the message stand out and be noticed. Using different colors for different family members can also be useful.

To Do List at Work

Keeping a constant To Do list going to remind yourself of jobs that need to be done at work can help you quickly decide what to do next, prevent boredom throughout the work day, and help you become more productive in less time.

Be sure to prioritize your list to use every minute of your workday. Have your list ready when needed.

Chapter Ten

Time

Create a Busy Bag for you and your kids, and keep it filled with fun things to do. Use it for long trips or going out to any place where you know you will be waiting around for a while.

For adults

Try filling it with magazines, books, knitting, or whatever else you would like to catch up on.

For young children (backpacks work best)

Try filling it with books and quiet toys and games such as dolls or action figures, playing cards, coloring books with crayons, crossword puzzles, and other brain-teasing games. If you feel the need to bring a small drink and snack, just remember water is best to avoid a sticky mess, and bite-size snacks are also less messy. Things to avoid: toys with small parts (these get lost easily), noisy items (these can disturb people around you), and do not bring a *good* book and crayons in the same bag (not a good idea with a small child; they will be sure to color it in no time).

70

Guilt

Guilt is usually one of the reasons we waste so much of our precious time. So why do we consistently feel guilty for simply not being able to be in two places at one time or for merely saying "no thank you" to yet another invitation?

Spreading our schedules too thin can cause major stress in our lives, and most of the time is just not worth it.

Prioritize your time; put yourself and your family first and do not waste precious time feeling guilty about not attending yet another function.

Multitasking and Saving Time

Believe it or not, multitasking isn't always a timesaver. It can even be dangerous if you are trying to multitask while doing things that need your full attention, such as driving a car or operating dangerous machinery.

Sometimes you need to concentrate only on the task at hand in order to get it done correctly and as quickly as possible the first time. When you don't need to concentrate completely on the task at hand, and it is safe to do so, multitasking can be a great time saver.

To save time, try planning ahead and using your time wisely. Here are a few timesaving ideas to consider:

1) Consolidate your errands into the least number of trips possible.

2) Use a planner to plan ahead.

3) Don't overextend and overcommit yourself.

4) Bring items with you (busy bag) to do when you are waiting at appointments, waiting for your kids, etc.

5) Consider getting up a few minutes earlier and use that time to get a few things done.

6) Purchase dishwasher-safe items when possible to help conserve water and avoid wasting time hand washing.

7) Purchase clothing that does not need professional dry cleaning (this saves both time and money).

8) Use television time to:

   a) Fold laundry.

   b) Update your shopping list.

   c) Clip and organize your coupons.

   d) Create a To Do list.

   e) Surf the internet.

   f) Exercise.

Multitask when you can and you will save lots of precious time.

Schedule It In

You would be surprised to find out how much time you have available to do those things you never seem to have time to do, if you only take the time to schedule it in. Mark it on your calendar, write yourself a note, get up an hour earlier, watch less television, spend less time on the computer—whatever it takes to schedule it in and set time aside to get it done.

Timesharing

Setting a timer or setting up a timesharing schedule for your family members to allot certain time frames for each person to use certain items or areas of the home can be extremely beneficial and save a lot of arguments.

Timesharing schedules can be used for sharing bathroom use, television time, game time, and much more. Allow for changes and adjustments as needed and agreed upon, and give everyone the option of exchanging time allotments if necessary.

Individualize

After each shopping trip, take time to individualize some of your items so you can quickly grab what you need, when you need it, without opening a box or package. If each item is already packaged in individual size packages, simply take each individual package and place it in an open container or basket for easier access. If they need to be separated into smaller portions, do so using small Ziploc bags or containers if necessary.

Cooking in bulk and freezing the extras when making dinner, pies, breads, and other foods can also save a lot of time.

See the following pages for more information:

1) "Grab and Go Snacks" (Chapter 19).

2) "Cook in Bulk and Freeze to Save Time and Effort" (Chapter 19).

Save Computer Time

Create your own list of keyboard shortcuts to help save computer time. Below is an example list of commonly used keyboard shortcuts:

1) Ctrl + A = Select all

2) Ctrl + C = Copy

3) Ctrl + F = Find

4) Ctrl + H = Find and replace

5) Ctrl + N = Open new program

6) Ctrl + O = Open saved program

7) Ctrl + P = Print the current page

8) Ctrl + V = Paste

9) Ctrl + W = Close the current window

10) Ctrl + X = Cut

11) Ctrl + Z = Undo

12) Ctrl + drag = Copy selected items

13) Ctrl + right arrow = Move to the next word

14) Ctrl + left arrow = Move to the previous word

15) Ctrl + down arrow = Move down to next paragraph

16) Ctrl + up arrow = Move up to the previous paragraph

17) Ctrl + shift + any arrow key = Highlight selected items

18) Ctrl + tab = Move forward through tabs

19) Ctrl + esc = Display the start menu

20) Ctrl + F4 = Close the current document

21) Ctrl + Home = Move to the first character

22) Ctrl + End = Move to the last character

23) Shift + Delete = Delete the item permanently by skipping the recycle bin

24) Shift + Any arrow key = Select text

25) Shift + F10 = Display the shortcut menu for the selected item

26) Alt + Tab = Switch between open items

27) Alt + Spacebar = Open the shortcut menu for the active window

28) Alt + Enter = View the properties for the selected item

29) Alt + F = File menu

30) Alt = F4 = Close the program

31) Win = Displays the start menu

32) Win + D = Switch between desktop and open programs

33) Win + E = Open My Computer

34) Win + F = Find

35) Win + F1 = Windows help

36) Win + L = Lock keyboard

37) Win + M = Minimize all windows

38) Win + Pause/Break = View basic information about your computer

39) Win + Shift + M = Restore all minimized windows

40) Win + R = Open Run dialog box

41) Win + Tab = Cycle through the items on the taskbar

42) Win + U = Open utility manager

43) F1 = Help menu

44) F5 = Find and replace

Chapter Eleven

Plan Ahead

Part of planning ahead is being prepared as much as possible. Here are a few questions you can ask yourself to make sure you are planning ahead:

1) Should I create a list? (Shopping list, reminder list, list of places to stop, etc.)

2) Do I have a reminder note posted where I will be sure to see it?

3) Did I leave the item out where I will see it so I will remember to bring it with me?

4) Do I have enough in stock so I don't have to make a sudden trip to the store?

5) Do I have a bag full of items I can be working on while I am out? Is it ready to go?

Set your clothes out for the next day, make tomorrow's lunch the night before, write a shopping list for your next trip to the store, stock up on supplies, have an emergency kit and emergency contact numbers available to all family members, write yourself reminder notes, leave a few minutes early, etc. Most of all: always expect and make time for the unexpected. If you think ahead, plan ahead, and prepare ahead of time, life will be more enjoyable and a lot less stressful.

Family Calendar

Keeping a schedule for the entire family organized and running smoothly can be a challenge. Family calendars are absolutely essential. Whether you have a traditional paper calendar or a calendar you can access online, a calendar the entire family can access is very important to help keep everyone informed and prevent schedule conflicts. For those who want to be able to access and check it from anywhere, an online calendar may be the best choice (Google has a nice online calendar available at www.google.com/calendar). For those who need a constant, once a day, visual reminder, a paper calendar may be a better choice.

Be Prepared and Stock Up

Keep your commonly used items in stock at all times. This includes food items (those that will not spoil or expire before they are used), toiletries, paper products, and office supplies. Every time you take an item and leave only one of that item left in stock, make it household policy to add the item to your shopping list. This way you have plenty of time before you *have* to purchase it again and you can stock up during your next shopping trip, when you find it for a good price.

This will also prevent running out of those much-needed items at the last minute, resulting in an unexpected trip to the store and wasting time, energy, gas, and money. Many people unnecessarily spend extra money on items they need because they cannot wait for a sale or better deal. If you keep your commonly used items in stock you will not be caught in this situation very often.

Gift Ideas and Preparation

To help avoid that last minute rush for a gift, some prep work may be necessary. Coming up with a gift idea and having the supplies needed to wrap it once the gift has been purchased can be stressful if you are not prepared ahead of time. There are several ways you can avoid this stress.

Keep a hidden Gift Ideas list going all year long, and add items to it every time you hear someone mention something they like or would like to have. Then when a birthday or other special occasion comes along, you will already have some gift ideas in mind for that person. Holidays, birthdays, and other special occasions will be a lot quicker and easier that year.

Keeping certain items in stock can also help to avoid last-minute runs to the store. Items you should always have on hand include gift bags, wrapping paper, bows, ribbon, tape, scissors, and a few extra gifts you know most people will enjoy. Having these items available can come in handy on those days when the unexpected happens and you've suddenly run out of time to go to the store.

With a little preparation your holidays, birthdays, and other special occasions can be a little less stressful and a lot more enjoyable.

TRIP LISTS

Before you leave for any trip, referring to a Do Before Leaving and Bring on Trip list can always be beneficial. Have these lists saved on your computer or printed and stored with your suitcases or travel gear so they are ready to use prior to any future trips.

Example list of things you may need to do before leaving and things you may need to bring with you:

Do Before Leaving

1) Book hotel, flight, rental car.

2) Plan and map out destinations.

3) Print map, update GPS (Global Positioning System).

4) Check weather forecast.

5) Stop mail and cancel any deliveries.

6) Water plants.

7) Do car maintenance.

8) Care for animals.

9) Set alarm system or arrange for a house-sitter.

10) Lock doors and windows and close curtains and shades.

11) Lock up or hide valuables and cash.

12) Make sure everything is shut off.

13) Place lights on a timer.

14) Unplug all electronics.

15) Turn down thermostat and water heater.

16) Shut off main water.

17) Inform family members of your itinerary and phone numbers where you can be contacted.

18) Pay any bills that will be due while gone.

19) Empty refrigerator of anything that will spoil while gone.

20) Clean all laundry and dishes.

21) Empty trash.

22) Set auto reply on any email correspondence if necessary.

23) Visit doctor for physical, update shots.

Bring On Trip

1) Clothes, shoes, boots, socks, underwear, slippers, pajamas.

2) Coat, gloves, hat, scarf.

3) Travel sewing kit.

4) Personal care and hygiene products.

   a) Soap, face wash.

   b) Toothpaste, toothbrush & mouthwash.

   c) Shampoo.

   d) Deodorant.

e) Lotion.

f) Makeup.

g) Shaving cream & razors.

h) Hairbrush, comb, hairspray, curling iron.

i) Q-tips.

j) Feminine hygiene products.

k) Tissues.

l) Hand sanitizer.

5) Vitamins and medications (prescriptions and others).

a) Motion sickness.

b) Pain killers.

c) Allergy medicine.

d) Antacids.

6) Passport and driver's license.

7) Credit cards, cash, traveler's checks.

8) Maps, GPS, printed directions, itinerary.

9) Emergency roadside kit.

10) Emergency first aid kit.

11) Sunglasses, sunscreen, bug spray, umbrella.

12) Fun stuff for the trip.

a) Beach towels and toys.

b) Sports equipment.

     c) Fishing equipment.

13) Fun stuff to do in the car.

     a) Portable TV or DVD player.

     b) Books.

     c) Small games and toys.

14) Snacks, drinks, cooler.

15) Bottle opener.

16) Adapter, batteries, charger.

17) Travel alarm.

18) Blankets, pillows.

19) Camera, camcorder.

20) Notebook, pens, pencils.

21) Plastic bags (garbage, Ziploc, etc.)

Having these lists ready for your next trip will always be beneficial, and saving them on your computer to easily update at any time makes maintaining them even easier.

Emergency Kits

Emergency kits need to be kept in easily accessible places so you are not tripping over things in the dark to get to them during an emergency situation.

Here are a few items you may want to have set aside in case of an emergency:

1) Canned and dried foods (with expiration dates as late as possible).

2) Bottled water.

3) First Aid kit.

   a) Bandages and sterile gauze pads.

   b) Medical tape.

   c) Antiseptic.

   d) Medications.

   e) Scissors.

   f) Tweezers.

   g) Thermometer.

4) Supplies.

   a) Can opener (non-electric).

   b) Pots, pans, cooking utensils.

   c) Paper plates, cup, dishes, and plastic utensils.

   d) Paper, pens, pencils.

   e) List of emergency contacts.

   f) Batteries.

   g) Flashlight, candles.

   h) Matches, lighter.

   i) Signal flare.

   j) Fire extinguisher.

k) Tape, rope.

l) Ziploc bags—all sizes.

m) Copies of any important documents such as birth certificates, marriage license, etc.

n) Pliers, screwdrivers, hammer, wrench.

Final Affairs in Order

Leaving a list of information for your loved ones at the time of your death will make things much easier during what will undoubtedly be a very difficult time for them.

Shown below is a simple checklist to help you prepare:

1) Prepare a power of attorney and health care proxy.

2) Prepare a will and include the following:

a) Name the executor for your will.

b) Your wishes for funeral arrangements. If funeral arrangements have already been made with a local funeral parlor, leave that information along with any additional instructions necessary.

c) Name beneficiaries for specific assets to be distributed such as cash, real estate, and personal belongings, and be sure to name the beneficiary who will receive the remaining assets. Include alternate beneficiaries for cases where the intended beneficiary is no longer living at the time of your death.

d) Name a guardian for your children.

e) Name a new owner for your pets.

f) Specify how debts and expenses should be paid, cancelled, etc.

3) Leave written instructions for anything necessary, such as home maintenance or special care for children or pets.

4) Leave a list of any memberships or subscriptions that may need to be cancelled.

5) Write down any needed information such as account numbers, account balances, contact information, etc. along with instructions on where to locate any important papers such as:

a) Last will and testament.

b) Life insurance policy.

c) Stocks, bonds.

d) Marriage certificate.

e) Prenuptial agreement.

f) Divorce papers.

g) Birth certificate.

h) Citizenship papers (if applicable).

i) Social security card.

j) Passport.

k) Military discharge papers.

l) Titles and deeds (automobile, real estate, etc.).

m) Personal paperwork.

n) Letters to loved ones.

o) Life insurance policies.

p) Disability claims (if applicable).

q) Retirement accounts.

r) Bank accounts.

s) Credit card accounts.

t) Mortgage.

u) Creditors.

Death of a Loved One

Remembering everything that has to be done can be extremely difficult when grieving the death of a loved one.

Shown below is a checklist of items to help you remember as much as possible:

1) Look for any instructions or important papers the deceased may have left behind. Below is a list of items you **may** need:

a) Death certificate (several certified copies will be needed).

b) Copy of will.

c) Copy of life insurance policy.

d) Birth certificate (of deceased and the children of the deceased).

e) Citizenship papers (if applicable).

f) Social security card.

g) Passport.

h) Marriage certificate.

i) Prenuptial agreement.

j) Divorce papers.

k) Military discharge papers.

l) Titles and deeds (automobile, real estate, etc.).

m) Stocks, bonds.

n) Personal paperwork.

o) Disability claims (if applicable).

p) Bank account numbers.

q) Most recent tax forms and W-2.

2) Notify family members, friends, and loved ones of the death.

3) Notify the funeral home of the death and make the necessary arrangements. This may or may not include decisions on the following:

a) Funeral home, time and location of service.

b) Type of religious services.

c) Burial or cremation, burial site.

d) Casket.

e) Clothes to be worn.

f) Eulogy.

g) Pallbearers.

h) Limousine service.

i) Music.

j) Flowers.

k) Where donations received will be sent.

4) Prepare an obituary for the local newspaper. Information you may need for the obituary:

a) Birth name and married name (if applicable).

b) Date of birth.

c) Name of survivors and those who have preceded them in death including:

    I. Mother and father.

    II. Spouse.

    III. Children, children's spouse's names.

    IV. Grandchildren.

d) Schools attended.

e) Armed service information.

f) Occupation.

g) Hobbies, interests, volunteer work (if applicable).

h) Funeral and calling hours information (times and locations).

i) Where donations, flowers, etc. should be sent.

5) If the deceased was a veteran, notify the funeral home of this information and contact the U.S. Department of Veterans Affairs: Phone: 1-800-827-1000, Website: www.va.gov, for any benefits and information available.

6) Obtain several copies of the death certificate from the funeral director.

7) If necessary, have mail forwarded and cancel memberships and subscriptions (magazine, newspaper, etc.).

8) If necessary, transfer ownership (titles, deeds, etc.) of the following:

a) Automobiles.

b) Real estate.

c) Stocks, bonds.

9) Notify companies, creditors, account holders, etc. of the death. You may need the following for each: account or policy numbers, copy of death certificate, or claim form.

a) Life insurance company.

b) Loved one's employer. Obtain information on any pension plans or death benefits.

c) Social Security (if they received Social Security benefits). If you are a surviving spouse ask about increasing benefits for yourself and any minor children.

d) All account holders, including accounts for the following:

    I. Stocks, bonds.

    II. Retirement accounts.

    III. Bank accounts.

    IV. Credit card accounts.

    V. Mortgage.

    VI. Creditors.

10) Make sure unpaid bills, taxes and debts from the deceased are satisfied.

11) File a final tax return for the deceased, if necessary.

A Great Quote to Remember:

"Fail to plan and you plan to fail."

Chapter Twelve

Finances

It is very important to keep track of your expenses and maintain a family budget. Knowing exactly how much money is coming in and going out each month can be extremely beneficial and is crucial to maintaining a healthy financial situation.

Start by keeping track of expenses for a month or more. This will give you a better idea of just how much you spend each month. Once you have done this, write down all expenses on paper or create a computer file (ready to print and update when necessary).

Next, add a list of future goals that will involve spending or saving money.

Here are two examples of a financial layout:

BUDGET: As of 1/1/2012

Debtor / Name of Expense	Next Due Date	Monthly Payment/Cost	Current Balance	A.P.R. / Notes	Loan Amount / Credit limit
Mortgage	1/1/2012	$903.00	$113,000.00	6.15%, 30 yrs.	$150,000
Home Equity Loan	1/5/2012	$242.00	$10,000.00	8.15%, 10 yrs./ Pay $542 ($300 extra)	$20,000
Car Loan	1/5/2012	$350.00	$6,000.00	7.5%, 5 yrs. / Pay $550 ($200 extra)	$19,000
Mastercard	1/6/2012	$0.00	$0.00	17.9% purchases/ 21.9% cash	$10,000
Visa	1/10/2012	$0.00	$0.00	15.9% purchases/ 19.9% cash	$5,000
Store Credit Card	1/21/2012	$0.00	$0.00	21%?	$1,500
Cell Phone Bill	1/10/2012	$155.00			
Television	1/11/2012	$80.00			
Heat / Air Conditioning	1/10/2012	$150.00			
Life Insurance	1/14/2012	$100.00		*AUTO DEDUCT FROM CHECKING ACCT*	
Car Insurance	1/15/2012	$84.00		*AUTO DEDUCT FROM CHECKING ACCT*/$1,008/yr.	
Garbage pickup	1/18/2012	$35.00			
Electric bill	1/26/2012	$330.00			
Food, gas, supplies, kids allowance		$1,200.00		$300 / wk.	
Prescriptions and doctor's visits		$100.00			
Kids school lunches		$200.00			
Investments		$200.00			
Property Taxes	9/31/2012	$333.00		$3,996 / yr.	
Extra money towards savings account	1/20/2012	$500.00			
Extra money towards paying off debt		$500.00		Work on paying off Home Equity Loan & Car Loan	
AAA	10/30/2012	$15.00		$180 / yr.	
	TOTAL:	$5,477.00	$129,000.00		$205,500

Bucket Lists

Wife

1) Travel abroad
2) Go on a cruise
3) Sky dive
4) Be debt-free by age 40

Husband

1) Retire by age 50
2) Travel
3) Learn a martial art
4) Run a marathon

Once you can see your finances laid out on paper, you will know exactly what your family budget should be. Then you will be able to make more informed decisions about your finances, which will result in much better outcomes.

Creating this financial layout on paper will also help you and your family:

1) Keep track of finances.

2) Quickly see any areas of concern.

3) Pay off debt quicker by scheduling in extra payments.

4) Plan for the future.

Maintain finances in a way that will help you stay on course to reach your financial goals as soon as possible.

Maintain this financial layout as often as possible and you will soon see positive results.

Designate an Area for Bill Paying

Immediately place incoming bills into this area. Store supplies within reach, including:

1) Envelopes

2) Calculator

3) Stamps

4) Pens and pencils

5) Return address labels or stamper

File paperwork immediately when you are done paying your bills.

Check All Statements Thoroughly

Everyone makes mistakes from time to time, including banks and credit card companies. Check for errors on statements and place a small checkmark by correct items to remind yourself that each one has been checked and is correct.

Tax Receipts

All tax receipts should be kept together in one file all year long, so when tax time comes around you will know where to find each one easily. If you have a lot of receipts, file them into separate folders by category and place those folders together.

If the information is not already on the receipt, write a small note somewhere on each receipt what was purchased, what or who it was for and any other useful information you may need for tax recordkeeping purposes.

Too Many Accounts

It may be time to consider consolidating accounts if:

1) You have piles of paperwork lying around that you haven't had time to deal with yet.

2) Bills haven't been paid because they were lost, put off to the last minute, or forgotten.

3) Certain tasks aren't being done because the paperwork is going to be too hard to find or is just too complicated.

Accounts you may want to consolidate include bank accounts, credit cards, loans, retirement plans, and investments. Fewer accounts mean less maintenance, less paperwork, and less chance for mistakes and lost revenue.

To help decide what accounts you should keep and what accounts to close, start with a list of all your accounts. Write down the pros and cons for keeping each account, such as what the account is costing you in fees, what the interest rates are, what the benefits are for keeping each account, etc. Once you have this written down, it should be easy to compare accounts and quickly decide which accounts to keep and which ones should be eliminated.

Once you have narrowed it down to the most important accounts, eliminate the ones that are no longer needed and consolidate the rest. This should cut down on the paper, confusion, errors, and stress.

Please keep in mind when closing any credit account that this will reduce the amount of your available credit and would increase the credit to debt ratio if a balance is carried. This ratio is reflected in your credit score.

Chapter Thirteen

Paperwork

It's funny how we keep hearing about a paperless society when most of us seem to be buried in paper on a daily basis. It's true that in some aspects we are reducing our use of paper and using digital content more and more, which is good for the environment. But at the same time, we seem to be living in a time when everything we do is requiring more and more paperwork to be filled out and filed.

If you do have piles of paper stacking up around your home there are several ways you can manage it. Listed on the next few pages are some tips to help you deal with those piles.

Eight Ways to Reduce or Eliminate Those Piles of Papers

1) Get a file cabinet and set up a filing system that works for you.

2) If you cannot file the papers away, separate them into categories and set up cubbies, shelves, or areas for each category of paper and continuously reevaluate whether or not that category of papers can be filed or

thrown away. If necessary, set up a separate file drawer for "Temporary," "Pending," or "Current Project" paperwork, just to help get it off of your desk.

3) Keep only the information you need to keep (see "Questions to Ask Yourself before Throwing Away Papers" below).

4) Scan it into your computer and save it. Or visit www.tryneat.com to see a scanning system that helps you save documents.

5) Go through mail immediately and take care of as much as possible.

6) Reduce what comes in. Stop bringing home paperwork you don't really need, cancel subscriptions, avoid signing up for mailings, etc.

7) Set aside a few minutes a day to tackle those piles of papers.

8) Purchase a paper sorter and organize by subject or category.

Questions to Ask Yourself Before Throwing Away Papers:

1) Do I need to keep this piece of paper?

2) Is the information outdated?

3) Is it useful information and could I possibly find the information again online?

4) Does it require attention? If so, why hasn't it been done yet and why not do it right away?

5) Is it an important document such as a birth certificate, marriage license, property deed, will, etc.?

6) Is it valuable or sentimental?

7) Would I be upset if it was lost in a fire?

8) What is the worst thing that could happen if I throw this away?

Once you have answered these questions, you should be able to determine whether or not you want to keep or throw away each piece of paper. And whatever you do decide to keep, be sure to file away.

What and When to Toss

There are many guidelines stating what to keep and when to toss different types of paperwork. Not all guidelines are exact and everyone's situation is unique. Keeping this in mind, I have always added some time to most guidelines to make sure I was not throwing anything out too soon. If you are not sure when to toss your important financial, legal, or business-related paperwork, check with your accountant or attorney before doing so.

Here is one guideline you can choose to follow or change as you see fit:

1) Papers you can throw away as soon as you sell, donate, or toss the item it refers to:

a) Vehicle titles.

b) Owner's manuals.

c) Warranties.

d) Instructions.

e) Loan documents (once the loan has been satisfied). Note: If you receive a letter stating the loan has been satisfied, be sure to keep this for seven years or more.

f) Sales receipts and related paperwork.

g) All property records, improvement receipts, etc.

2) Papers you can throw away when you receive an updated replacement:

a) Social security statements.

b) All insurance policies, such as:

    I. Auto.

    II. Home.

    III. Life.

    IV. Health.

3) Papers to keep for 1 to 3 years (or until you reconcile with your monthly statement):

a) Store receipts.

b) Credit card statements and receipts.

c) Investment statements.

d) Bank statements, deposit slips, and ATM receipts.

e) Phone bills.

f) Utility bills.

g) Medical bills.

Keep in mind, if any of these items are needed for proving a deduction for your federal or state tax returns you will need to file them with your tax records to keep for up to seven years or more.

4) Papers to keep for seven years or more: State and federal tax returns with supporting documents and receipts such as:

a) Bank statements for savings and checking account.

b) Credit card statements.

c) Sales receipts.

d) Large purchase and sale records: Property, stocks, bonds, etc.

e) Expense records: Phone bills, utility bills, repair bills, travel and entertainment.

f) Settlement claims.

g) Pay stubs and salary records (keep for seven years or until you reconcile with your W-2).

h) Investment paperwork: (keep until you sell the investment or empty the account, then an additional seven years with your tax records: retirement, pension plan, 401K, IRA papers)

i) All business-related income and expenses

5) Papers to keep forever: These should be kept in a fireproof box or a safe deposit box.

a) Birth certificate.

b) Citizenship papers.

c) Passports.

d) Social Security card.

e) Death certificate.

f) Marriage license.

g) Adoption papers.

h) Prenuptial agreements.

i) Divorce decrees.

j) Alimony and child custody agreements.

k) Military discharge records.

l) Wills, trusts, power of attorney

m) Life insurance policies (keep until the policy has ended).

n) Health care proxy.

o) Power of attorney.

p) Deeds and property titles.

q) Employer benefits plan documentation.

Double up Your Filing System

Try using both hanging and regular (non-hanging) file folders together. This way every time you take a file out of the file cabinet, you leave an empty hanging file behind and when you return the file you will know exactly where to place it (in the empty hanging file).

This also helps when you want to group files together. Here are a few examples of grouping files together:

In a hanging file folder, place regular files for:

1) All vehicles and car insurance; label it "Vehicles"

2) Your mortgage papers and homeowner's insurance; label it "House Information"

3) Large household appliances; label it "Large Appliances"

4) All family members; label it "Family Members"

5) All pets; label it "Pets"

6) Tax return files for several years; label it "Taxes"

7) All credit cards; label it "Credit Cards"

Continue this pattern with all files. Note: It is not necessary to label *all* hanging files, only those that contain a group of files.

Computer Folders

Computer information needs to be organized too. Create folders to store your emails, files, and pictures. Categorize them by subject and file each item immediately. If you decide you do not want to keep an item, delete it immediately. Regularly schedule computer maintenance and go through your emails, computer files, and pictures often, deleting what you no longer want and filing the rest.

How to Keep up With Incoming Mail

Deal with each piece of mail as soon as it comes in. Do not let it pile up or it can quickly become an overwhelming task and important items may be overlooked. Take your mail each day and stand over a recycling bin or garbage can and sift through it immediately, getting rid of the junk mail first and filing and sorting the rest. For security purposes, anything you are throwing away that has personal information on it should always be shredded.

Make sure bills are taken out and placed with other unpaid bills. Some people like to mark the bills immediately with the due date and amount due on the outside of each envelope so they know at a quick glance how much is due and when. If you do this, try writing the information on the very end of each envelope and sort them by due date, then set up a schedule (maybe one day each week) to pay your bills, and stick to that schedule.

If you notice the same junk mail or magazines coming in the mail day after day, take the time to request that they take you off their mailing list. This will help reduce the amount of incoming mail you have to deal with on a daily basis and also helps to save paper, postage, time, and resources.

If you make it part of your routine to deal with incoming mail on a daily basis, it becomes much easier to manage.

Make Time to Read Those Articles

Magazines can pile up fast. Do you have magazines piling up somewhere in your home? The magazines you swear you are going to have time to read someday? If so, try taking some time (perhaps when you are sitting in front of the television at night) to skim through those magazines and pull out the articles you are interested in reading. Place them in a pocket folder and the next time you have to go to an appointment or attend a function where you know you will be sitting around waiting for a while, bring this folder with you. Try leaving it in the car for those unexpected times when you could use something to read.

If you only have a few magazines, just bring the magazines with you instead. When you are done with the magazine, simply recycle it or consider passing it along to someone who may also enjoy it.

Finding Your Receipts

Finding the correct receipt when needed can be a challenge if you don't have a filing system in place for incoming receipts. Receipts should immediately be filed in one of two places, depending on whether you paid cash or used a credit or debit card to pay for your purchases.

All receipts reflecting cash payments should be filed away immediately. Receipts reflecting payments using a credit or debit card should be stored in an area next to incoming mail, statements, and unpaid bills until they have been checked against the statement. Once the statement has been checked against the purchases listed on the receipt, if everything is correct and the amounts match, place a small checkmark on the top of the receipt. If your statement arrives in paper format, mark the charge on the statement as well. This will remind you that you have already checked that particular charge and it was correct. Once the totals match and there are no returns to be made, it is then time to file or toss your receipt, whichever is appropriate.

For large purchases such as major appliances, and other receipts you would like to keep for years to come, file the receipts in a properly labeled file with any paperwork that came with the item, including owner's manuals, warranties, etc.

All other receipts that are to be kept for a shorter period of time should be stored in a small box just large enough to accommodate about one years' worth of receipts, such as a shoebox, photo box, or any other small container you may have handy.

Make sure to label your box "Receipts" so it can be easily identified and found by other family members when needed.

Sort them in the box in a way that works best for you and your family. You can place them in a pile (placing the newest receipts on the top of the pile and the oldest receipts at the bottom), or you can create a miniature filing system by using large, brightly colored index cards that you have labeled. Separate them by store name, type of store, or type of items purchased (Grocery, Home Improvement, Clothing, Gas, Other), filing the oldest receipts in the back and the newest ones in the front or the other way around.

When the box starts to get full, it is then time to go through the oldest receipts and decide which ones can be thrown away and which ones need to be kept a little longer.

Finding your receipts when needed should be much easier once this filing system is in place.

Storage of Your Pending Receipts

Pending receipts (receipts waiting to be checked against a statement) can pile up and become messy if they are simply tossed into a box, drawer, or left in a pile on your desk. Either store them in separate labeled envelopes (one for each account) or simply place them into a pocket folder.

One example: one side can be used for checking account receipts and the other side can be used for credit card receipts. Note: If you have a lot of pending receipts at one time, you can use more than one folder to separate each type of account.

Be sure to place the newest ones to the back of the folder or envelope behind the older ones (this will enable you to quickly take hold of the oldest ones first when checking them against your statement). Once you have checked each receipt, file or toss if necessary.

Tackle That Drawer Full of Papers

Do you have a drawer that is a catchall for miscellaneous paperwork; a drawer full of papers you just don't know what to do with? If so, it may be time to go through those papers.

Start by throwing out anything you no longer want or need.

Next, take out any important paperwork such as bills, important documents, receipts, etc. and place each one into its proper area or file.

Separate the remaining paperwork you still need to deal with into categories and place each category of paperwork into labeled pocket folders or file folders.

Here are a few categories that may be useful;

1) Saved articles and clippings you intend to read (once you read them, throw them out immediately or file them away).

2) Information (if you have several papers regarding one subject of information, create a separate folder for each subject).

3) Current Projects.

4) Pending items that need attention. If some are urgent, create a separate file for the urgent ones or simply sort them in the folder by rate of urgency, one in front of the other.

Once the remaining paperwork has been separated into pocket folders or file folders, they can then be filed away into a separate "Pending" file drawer, or you can simply place them neatly back into the drawer they came out of until you have more time to deal with each one.

Placing these papers into files or file folders makes it much easier for you to simply grab each one and take it with you wherever you go. This gives you more options for where and when you will be able to deal with each one, whether it's in the car, at an appointment, or simply sitting in front of the television. Having the ability to simply grab the folder and take it with you wherever you go gives you many more opportunities to go through the paperwork whenever you have the available time to do so.

Highlight and Bold

Highlighting important information and separate categories of information, whether it is on paper or in a document saved on the computer, can be a huge time saver when having to reread any document.

It helps you find the correct information much quicker and can save you from having to reread an entire document.

You can also save lots of time by immediately scaling down any document before you save it on the computer. Simply delete all sentences you will not need before you save the document. This way the information you need in the document can be easily found.

Chapter Fourteen

Family Communication

Most families today are so busy they don't have enough time to communicate with each other. Communication is very important in preventing stress, arguments, frustration, wasted time, and wasted resources. Designating a communication area somewhere inside your home can help tremendously in keeping everyone in the family well informed, well organized, and working together.

This communication area should be in a place everyone walks by each day. It should also be in a place where everyone can pick up or distribute belongings, pick up or leave notes and reminders, check off To Do lists, and check schedules.

This area should have an erasable board or bulletin board for posting notes and other items, pens, pencils, sticky notes or paper for writing notes, and a family calendar for keeping track of family members' schedules and events. You should also have an area (maybe just a table or cleared surface to work on) to place lost, misplaced, or miscellaneous items.

Suggested items to keep in any family communication area include (but should not be limited to): To Do lists, chore sheets, family calendar, items to be distributed, notes, reminders, schedules, incoming mail to be distributed, and clean clothes to be distributed to each family member's room. Basically, anything you need to communicate, share, or distribute to other members of your family should be kept in this area.

Some places you may want your communication area to be might be an office, entryway, hallway, mudroom, or laundry room. The important thing to remember is that it should be in a common place in the home where everyone in the family will be walking through on a daily basis. After a while, everyone will know where to leave notes or items and where to go for what they need, and communication should no longer be a problem.

Post Important Information Where It Is Needed Most

Posting important information in the correct area is critical if you want the information to be used when needed. Kids' school schedules, morning checklists, and chore sheets should be on a magnetic board near their desk in their room. Stain remedies should be posted inside a cabinet somewhere in the laundry room. Information and instructions for medications, vitamins, diets, and natural cure remedies should be inside the cabinet door where you store medications and vitamins.

If you have more than one sheet of information, try posting them one on top of the other so all you have to do is lift each one to see the information posted underneath.

More important information such as emergency numbers, reminder notes, appointment cards, and schedules should be posted in an area where they are more visible to everyone. Try using a magnetic erasable board placed in an area of the home where everyone will see it. In my opinion these are better than corkboards because they can be wiped clean and usually don't look worn out after years of use. Magnetic clips are great to use on these because you can hang many items at once.

Dinner Time

Dinner time is a great time to get your family together. It's also a great time to start planning ahead. You can plan and discuss upcoming events, appointments, family vacations, the family schedule, and upcoming meals. Get out the family calendar to make sure everyone's schedules will work together and write down any plans. And don't forget to add the items you will need for any upcoming meals or plans to your shopping list.

Information for Each Folder

Posting reminders of important information where it can easily be found is always helpful and can be a great time saver.

When using folders to file information away, place Post-it notes or simply write inside the front section of each folder to help remind you of any important information regarding the folder.

Chapter Fifteen

Organizing Your Kids

K ids Need to Be Organized Too! This Includes Schedules, Chores, and Rules.

Start kids out early with good organizational habits and teach them how to keep up with daily life. Give them storage containers to use and show them where to store each item. Teach them how to keep a schedule, calendar, and daily checklists, and have them write down daily reminder notes for those constantly forgotten items. If they earn money, show them how to create a budget to track their savings and expenses.

When developing chore sheets and rule sheets, try to be creative and add in something fun to help keep each child's interest. Most importantly, make each child responsible for his or her own responsibilities, but continue to monitor their progress as well. Children tend to stray from their responsibilities from time to time, so a checklist can help children, as well as parents, monitor their achievements.

When chores, rules, and reminders are all clearly written down, most parents will be surprised at how cooperative,

114

enthusiastic, and proud a child can be when he or she has completed everything. This teaches them responsibility as well as great organizational skills. And, of course, positive reinforcement and the occasional reward help keep this feeling going.

It may also help to have an Extra Jobs list handy. This would be a list of extra jobs available to your child if they want to do some extra work around the house to help out and possibly earn extra privileges. This is also a great way for a child to earn extra money towards that specific item he or she has been saving for.

Don't wait—help teach your kids responsibility and organization today. The more they learn today, the better off they will be tomorrow.

Twenty Ways to Get Your Child to Pick Up and Organize Their Bedroom—and Keep it That Way

1) "A place for everything and everything in its place." If you notice that certain items are not put away properly, help your child find a place to store them. Most children have trouble keeping their room clean because they have not yet established a place to store each item.

2) Set a timer and challenge them to find ten items to pick up and put away in ten minutes. And give them incentives to do more, such as a special treat or extra privilege for each additional ten items.

3) Challenge them to find ten items to give away, throw away, or sell. Or provide them with a box to fill with unwanted items. If they are asking to go to the store to purchase a special item, this is the perfect opportunity

to have them make room for that new item by getting rid of some older, unused items.

4) Make it a standing rule that for each new item going into their room, one has to come out. Examples: One toy in; one toy out. One piece of clothing in; one piece of clothing out.

5) Make it part of their daily chores to pick up their room at the end of each day. Follow up with inspections. Establish a rule that privileges and rewards will always be on hold until all chores are done.

6) Make rules and consequences for certain areas of your child's bedroom and make sure to follow through with each rule. Example: Desks are for schoolwork only; no toys allowed on the desk or they will be taken away for a few days.

7) Give incentives such as an allowance, special privileges, extra game time with Mom or Dad, a new toy or game, their choice of dinner, extra television or computer time, etc. These can all be incentives for cleaning their rooms. Get creative and find what works for you and your child.

8) Work together to help your child organize what they have. Give them ideas on how to organize each set of items and help them come up with ideas of their own. For example: pens and pencils in a cup, homework papers separated into folders labeled by subject, stuffed animals on a shelf or stored in a large basket or container, toy cars in a container marked "toy cars."

116

Challenge them to come up with ideas of their own by asking what container or which area of their room they should store each set of items in.

9) Make sure they have plenty of space for storage and plenty of storage containers to use. Let them use a label maker to help label and organize their things. Purchase a new toy chest, storage containers, or special organizers if necessary, or simply give your child a box he or she can decorate and use.

10) Provide plenty of shelving for displaying items, storing toys, books, CDs, movies, and more.

11) Be clear on what needs to be done and give specific, written instructions so they can check off each item they have finished. Example: make the bed, clean off your desk, vacuum the rug, go through your clothes and get rid of the ones that no longer fit or you no longer want, empty the garbage can, pick up the toys off the floor, etc. (Tip: Save this list on your computer so you or your child can print it out the next time it's needed).

12) Set the rules ahead of time and be clear on how your child should and should not clean the room. Examples: dust the shelf before placing items back on it, no shoving things under the bed or in the back of the closet. Let them know you will be inspecting these areas when they are done.

13) Be positive and encouraging every time you check their progress. Try to find something to compliment

them on each time and offer plenty of words of encouragement and praise.

14) Provide a small laundry basket to keep in their room for dirty clothes, and have them be responsible for bringing their own dirty laundry to the laundry room when it is full.

15) Let them play their favorite music to help keep them upbeat while picking up and cleaning.

16) Have your child work on one category of items at a time: clothes first, stuffed animals second, paper and pencils third, etc. Or make it a game by having them pick up one color of items at a time: blue items first, green items second, red items third, etc.

17) Have your child eat a healthy meal prior to the clean-up, and establish break times, if any, before the clean-up begins. No one can work well on an empty stomach.

18) No excuses: Explain the reason for the mess and how they can prevent it from becoming such a large mess the next time. Let them come up with some ideas of their own.

19) Make it easy to clean up by giving them open containers to quickly toss items into, and have them hang or stack as many clothes as possible (clothes tend to get lost and forgotten about in drawers and it takes longer when children have to take time to fold each item).

20) Help your child decorate their room in a way they will enjoy; this creates the incentive of keeping the room picked up and looking nice.

Helping your child learn how to pick up and keep their room organized can help reduce their stress level as well as your own, and makes the clean-up process a fun and positive experience which benefits everyone.

Chore Sheets

Chore sheets are essential and help your child remember what needs to be done and when, so write it down on paper to help them stay organized.

CHORES SHEET

Name: _____

Date: _____ to _____

Rules: Write down excuse if you cannot do a chore. For each day that chores are not done and no excuse is written, you lose $1.00/day and you will need to do one additional chore for the person who did your chore for you (their choice).

Chores marked with "XXXX" do not have to be done that day. If chores are not done and marked as done, you will NOT be paid for them.

Money Earned: Reward money and extra work done: can be used for spending and/or put into your savings account.

Chore money: half can be used for spending and half has to go into your savings account.

Rewards:	Pay Rate	Sun	Mon	Tue	Wed	Thurs	Fri	Sat
For each test or quiz 90 or above	.50 each							
For each test/quiz 100 or above	$1.00 each							
One week getting up with alarm by yourself	$ .50 each							
Did all chores, every day, all week long	$1.00 extra							

Extra Work Done This Week:_____ **Amount Earned:** _____

Chores: Pay rate: $7.00/week	Sun	Mon	Tue	Wed	Thurs	Fri	Sat
Study/Do Homework	xxxx						
Put away clothes/set out ones for next day							
Clean your room	xxxx		xxxx		xxxx		
Feed dog & cat							
Empty upstairs hamper	xxxx	xxxx		xxxx	xxxx	xxxx	
Vacuum rugs							xxxx
Take your vitamin		xxxx	xxxx	xxxx	xxxx	xxxx	xxxx
15 minutes of reading	xxxx			xxxx			xxxx
Take out the garbage and recyclables	xxxx		xxxx	xxxx	xxxx	xxxx	xxxx

Morning Checklist:

Check your....... schedule, calendar and/or checklist

Do you have.......your homework, lunch money, gym clothes and library book?

If you have extra time in the morning.......study for a test, do some chores or read a book.

Did you........eat breakfast and brush your teeth?

Job Cards for Kids

Job cards are a fun, competitive way for kids to earn some extra money or rewards. It's also a great way to get those chores done that everyone seems to be too busy to do. By using job cards, everyone will have the privilege of doing the chores listed on the cards at their convenience.

Here's how it works: Choose any blank business-size cards or index cards. On each card, write down the job that needs to be done and how much you are willing to pay to have it done. If you don't want to pay for the job to be done, offer some kind of reward such as extra television time, one extra snack at bedtime, one item of their choice at the store, etc. If you have jobs listed that should only be for specific children, write down the names of the children they are intended for on the front of each card.

Examples:

Card #1: *Job Available: Wash the car*
Pay: $5.00
Job Available To: Joseph

Card #2: *Job Available: Sweep floors*
Reward: Your choice of one item at the store up to $3.00
Job Available To: Everyone

Card #3: *Job Available: Vacuum rugs*
Pay or Reward: $3.00 or one extra hour of television time
Job Available To: Everyone

Post the cards where the entire family can see them: on a magnetic board using magnetic clips (maybe near a Help Wanted sign), placed in a basket, or displayed like Christmas cards. When each job is done, have the child place the card into a different basket or small container so they can be used again when needed.

Let them know the job card rules, such as: the first one to take the card and start the job gets to earn the amount of money or reward stated on the card, and they are not allowed to take the card unless they are starting the job right away. This way it becomes a competition to see who can get the best jobs first and earn the most. When the job is done, they hand in the card for their money or reward. This gives the parent time to inspect the work that was done and see if the child has done a satisfactory job and earned the money or reward stated on the card.

Rule Sheets

Any family that has children can benefit from having a written set of rules. Writing household family rules down on paper makes it clear to everyone just what the rules are, so there is no question what needs to be done and what is or is not acceptable.

When creating your family rules sheet it can be helpful to include a sense of humor.

Some items you may want to include on your rule sheet:

1) Allowance and gift money amounts:

a) Clearly state the amount they will get paid at what age.

    b) When they will get paid (what day of the week, or whenever it is convenient for the parents).

    c) How the child can earn more money (have a list of extra jobs available).

    d) How they can earn rewards (Have a list of details such as: each good test score above 90 earns $1.00 or quarterly grades in school of 90 or above = $10 each).

    e) If the money is for spending or saving.

2) Chores:

    a) What chores need to be done.

    b) The rewards for getting them done.

    c) The consequences for not getting them done on time.

3) Computer and television rules: Time allotted for use and what needs to be done before using each one.

4) Healthy eating habits:

    a) What and how many are allowed.

    b) When snacks are allowed.

    c) Where in the home they are allowed to be consumed.

5) Bedtime: list a time for each child or each age.

6) Complaints: State if the child needs to write it down and place it in a complaint box, or if there is a specific time for complaints to be heard.

Family Rules

Revised 3/1/2013

Rules: Are subject to change at any time!

Money: Paydays are whenever we have time!

Pay is as follows:

> 10 yrs. old: $2.25 wk.
>
> 11 yrs. old: $2.50 wk.
>
> 12 yrs. old: $3.00 wk.
>
> 13 yrs. old: $3.50 wk.
>
> 14 yrs. old: $4.00 wk.
>
> 15 yrs. old: $5.00 wk.
>
> 16 yrs. old: $6.00 wk.
>
> 17 yrs. old: $7.00 wk.

High school graduation: Get a job, attend college, or both!

1) Every week half of your pay goes into your bank account and half is for you to spend.

2) Money can also be earned by extra work approved by Mom or Dad (see extra jobs list). Half always goes into the bank.

3) All fines and rewards come out of or go towards your spending money, and no fines will ever be taken out of money that is reserved for your bank account.

4) You can add extra money to your bank account at any time.

5) Half of any gift money goes towards your bank account.

6) You can earn reward money for good test and homework scores. This can be used toward spending money or your bank account—it's up to you.

   a) Making honor roll (average of 85-89) is $20.00.

   b) Making high honor roll (average of 90 or above) is $30.00.

   c) Student of the month awards are $5.00 each.

   d) End of quarter grades: A = $2.00 each, B = $1.00 each. F = You owe Mom and Dad $5.00 each.

Our school's grading system is as follows: **A**: 93-100, **B**: 85-92, **C**: 77-84, **D**: 70-76, **F**: 69 and below.

Chores will be done on time every day or you will be fined the amount shown on your chore sheet, or you will have to do an extra chore for each one not done. You will not have to do a chore **ONLY** if there has been an **X** marked over the space on your chores sheet ahead of time. If you were not here all day, write down "NOT HERE."

Computer and television rules

TV time starts at 7 pm only if homework and chores are done and marked off, unless Mom or Dad says otherwise. Computer time is only allowed on non-school days unless Mom or Dad says otherwise.

Soda: Only one glass a day maximum.

Snacks: No more than two non-healthy snacks allowed per night. *No snacks after bedtime.* Snacks will be finished and put away 15 minutes prior to bedtime. After that only one cup of water for your room at night is allowed, and the cup needs to be put away in the sink in the morning. No dirty dishes or food allowed in bedrooms.

Bedtime: 9 pm on school nights. 11 pm other nights.

Getting ready for bed and brushing your teeth will be done 15 minutes before bedtime.

ALL COMPLAINTS MUST BE HANDWRITTEN

Jobs List for Kids

Providing a list of available jobs, whether it's on job cards, a spreadsheet, or handwritten, is a great way to inspire your kids to get up and get some work done to help out and even earn some extra cash.

List available jobs such as mowing the lawn, sweeping out the garage, taking out the garbage, washing windows, or shoveling snow.

Make sure to include rules on this job sheet such as:

1) Trading rules (whether or not trading jobs is allowed among siblings).

2) Who the jobs are available to. Be sure to list the name of the child or age group next to each available job.

3) Whether or not a parent has to inspect the work before the child gets paid and whether or not the pay will be based upon job performance.

Provide them with a copy of the list of jobs and highlight or circle the ones they can or need to do each day.

"Extra Jobs" List:

Attention all kids: Earn extra money now!

If you would like to make extra money—occasionally Mom and Dad are willing to pay to have the following jobs done:

1) Weed garden, or dig up or pull weeds out of the lawn.

2) Brush or comb out the dog.

3) Mow or rake the lawn (for ages 12 and older).

4) Wash the walls.

5) Clean the bathroom.

6) Organize and clean up the garage.

7) Organize and clean up the cellar.

8) Wash floors.

9) Clean the car.

10) Wash windows.

11) Shovel snow.

12) Cut and file coupons.

13) Dust.

14) Bring in wood (for ages 12 and older).

15) Babysitting: $40 week (for ages 16 and older).

You can also trade one of these jobs for a chore you do not want to do.

If you are interested in one of these jobs ask Mom or Dad.

All pay rates will be based on job performance.

Thank you,

The management—Mom and Dad

Have a "Fun Things to Do" List Ready to Go

For whenever you or your children have free time and can't think of what to do for fun. These can also come in handy for children who are stuck at home and often bored. Tell them to come up with one on their own and add to it as much as possible.

Below are some sample lists of fun things to do. Mix and match the lists and add to them as often as possible.

Some examples for a "Fun things to do while at home" list for kids:

1) Draw (with crayons or chalk) a picture for someone in the family.

2) Decorate a large cardboard box.

3) Make a tent using a table and a sheet; camp out in the living room.

4) Write a thank you note.

5) Write a story or poem.

6) Set up an obstacle course.

7) Create a game to play.

8) Play a board game.

9) Read a book.

10) Play Wii fitness game or exercise.

11) Play with a family pet.

12) Build a fort.

13) Bake something (with adult supervision, of course).

14) Roller skating, roller blading, scooter.

15) Ride a bike.

16) Fly a kite.

17) Jump rope.

Example for a "Fun things to do list" for families or parents:

1) Bowling.

2) Girls or guys night out.

3) Dinner out.

4) Movies.

5) Golf.

6) See a game.

7) See a show.

8) Go on a picnic.

9) Go to the park.

10) Go to the beach.

11) Fishing.

12) Boating.

13) Visit the zoo.

14) Put together a jigsaw puzzle.

15) Garden.

16) Join a club.

17) Horseback riding.

18) Travel.

If you hadn't already noticed—I didn't add items like watch television, play on the computer, or anything else some of us do way too much already. The reason I didn't add those things is because the purpose of this list is to remind everyone of the fun things they seem to forget about and don't do often enough. Having these lists ready to go can help remind you of those things you love to do. To some people it may seem silly to keep such a list, but trust me when I say: It comes in handy!

Leaving Your Children Home Alone

Leaving children home alone can be extremely stressful to both the parents and the child, especially if the child is left with nothing to do for the day. Once your child reaches a suitable age to be left home alone, providing necessary guidelines for them to follow is usually necessary. It can also be very beneficial to leave a prepared list of things they should be doing while you are gone. Make sure to include enough to keep them busy the entire time, allow for break times, and include some fun ideas for when they are done with their list.

Some examples:

1) Read for thirty minutes.

2) Sweep.

3) Dust.

4) Wash windows.

5) Play a board game with your brother or sister.

6) Do your chores.

7) Write me a short story or poem.

8) Eat breakfast or lunch.

9) Check in with Mom or Dad at work at noontime.

10) Clean your room.

11) Fifteen minutes of exercise.

12) Feed and water pets.

13) No arguments with your brother or sister.

14) SMILE

15) One hour of television time or electronic game time if everything else has been done and marked off your list.

Remember—the more you have written down on paper, the better. This also includes a list of *household rules* for when you are not home such as:

1) Do not answer the phone unless you know it's Mom or Dad calling (Example: they hear Mom or Dad's voice on the answering machine or verify the identification of the caller as Mom or Dad).

2) Do not answer the door for anyone or let anyone in the house.

3) If you do end up talking to someone, do not let them know you are home alone. Always tell them Mom or Dad is busy or sleeping and cannot come to the door or phone.

4) Do not use the stove.

5) Keep windows and doors locked at all times.

6) Stay in the house at all times.

7) No friends are allowed to come over.

Having a list of emergency contacts available and going over what to do in the event of an emergency is also very important. Make sure your children know where fire extinguishers, first aid, and emergency kits are located, and update them so they are prepared to use them in the event of an emergency.

Organize Your Life and More ~ Christina Scalise

Make sure the lines of communication are always open and always ask your children about any concerns they may have. The more prepared you both are, the less stressful it will be to leave your child home alone.

Back to School

Sending your children back to school can be stressful if there is no preparation done ahead of time.

Here are a few things you can do to prepare and assure a smooth transition on the first day back to school:

1) Schedule doctor and dentist appointments prior to the first day of school.

2) Have your children try on all clothing to see what can still be worn throughout the year and what will need to be purchased.

3) One week before school starts, start conditioning your children to starting an early schedule. No more sleeping in.

4) If you have a list of school supplies needed for the year, make sure you shop for needed supplies as soon as possible.

5) If household chore sheets need to be updated to accommodate new school schedules, update them as soon as possible and review any new chores with your children if necessary.

6) Prepare a place for your children to do homework, and set up a filing system for any school papers.

Don't Forget the Homework

Designate a certain spot or area for your child to place his or her homework, gym clothes, and other school-related items every single day. This can be in the child's bedroom or somewhere else in your home, as long as they will be walking by it every day. Make sure you tell your child that if they are not currently working on it or using it, it has to be stored in this same area at all times, so they will not forget it when needed. You can also have an extra-large storage box with the child's name on it, or a cubby-type area to store these school related items (you or your child could also decorate it). Do whatever you think will work best for you and your child.

A morning and afternoon checklist should also be posted right next to this area, one your child can quickly read every morning and afternoon to make sure they are not forgetting anything. If you use an erasable board or chalkboard for this checklist, they can also update it at any time and include reminders for the next day. If you make it part of their everyday routine, it also becomes easier to remember.

Having a planner in school that lists everything that needs to be done or remembered, including homework assignments, is also essential so your child remembers to bring home everything that will be needed that night.

No matter what the age, trying to remember everything you need without writing it down is always risky. The busier we are, the more chance there is to forget that one needed item; forgetting that one item can make the difference in getting good grades or bad grades and having a good day or a bad day.

Planning for the Future

Make sure your children are planning for the future by giving them a budget they can work with, whether it's a simple budget to help your youngest child figure out how to save up for a toy he or she wants, or simply to get them thinking and planning for their future.

It is up to each parent to decide when each child is ready to receive the proper information. I have shown two examples of budgets below. One was written for young children, and one for teenagers. Please keep in mind that these are just examples and every child will need to have their personal budgets adjusted to match their personal needs. Some children may not be ready to start thinking about future expenses; keep this in mind when choosing how to set up your child's budget.

(Example Budget For Young Children): As of 1/1/2012

Name of Expense	Next Due Date	Today's Monthly Payment / Cost	Amount Still Owed	Original Loan Amount
Add Money to Savings Account	2/1/2012	$10.00		
Borrowed Money from Mom & Dad	2/1/2012	$10.00	$10.00	$20.00
Saving Money for new game		$5.00		
	TOTAL:	$25.00	$10.00	$20.00

Allowance and Other Income:
$5.00 a week allowance –
Half has to go into savings account & half is for spending.

$2.50 a week for doing extra jobs

Income vs. Debt:
Total Monthly Allowance & Income: $30.00
(Minus) Monthly Spending Amount: – $25.00
(Equals) Monthly Amount Left Over: $5.00

Financial Goals:
Save $30.00 for new game: $25.00 Saved so far
Earn an extra $100.00 by doing extra jobs and
add it to my saving account before next year.

Investments:	Current Balance
Current Stocks / Bonds Value:	$500.00
Savings Account Balance:	$2,000.00
College Account Balance:	$10,000.00
Total Investments:	$12,500.00

Things I Want To Do
Go To College

Organize Your Life and More ~ Christina Scalise

(Example Budget For Teenagers): As of 1/1/2012

Debtor / Name of Expense	Next Due Date	Today's Monthly	During College Monthly	Possible After College/ Monthly	Possible Future Monthly	Current Balance	Annual Percentage Rate (A.P.R.)/ Notes	Original Loan Amount/ Credit limit
Cell phone	2/1/2012	$10.00	$10.00	$100.00				
Food, gas, supplies				$1,200.00			(apx. $350/wk.)	
College meals / meal card			$250.00					
Mortgage / rent				$700			apx. 6% for 20-30years	
Car Loan				$386			apx. 5.99% for 6 years	$20,000.00
College Loans				$500			apx. 6.8% apr (unsubsidized)	
Credit card (Visa, Mastercard, American Express, Store)			$0.00			$0.00	*Always pay off every month*	
TV – (Cable, Satellite)				$75.00				
Movie rentals				$22.00				
Fuel Costs – Heat/A.C.				$150.00				
Life Insurance				$75.00				
Car Insurance				$83.33			(apx. $1,000/yr)	
Home Owner's Insurance					$83.33		(apx. $1,000/yr)	
Garbage service / pickup				$35.00				
Electric bill				$300.00				
Kids (after school activities, chores, lunches, etc.)					$300.00			
Prescriptions and doctor's visits copays				$100.00				
Medical insurance				$250.00				
Property Taxes — (town & county, school)					$250.00		apx. $3,000/yr.	
Add extra $ to savings account/pay off debt early		$70.00					(As much as you can afford)	
AAA					$14.83		apx. $178/yr.	
TOTAL:		$80.00	$260.00	$3,976.33	$648.16	$0.00		$20,000.00

Income / Paychecks:
$100.00 / week from weekend job
$40.00 / week allowance

Income vs. Debt:
Total Monthly Income:	$140.00
(Minus) Monthly Spending Amount:	–$80.00
(Equals) Monthly Amount Left Over:	$60.00

Other Possible Upcoming Expenses:
College, books, car maintenance / Wedding
New Car
Investments / Savings acct.

Financial Goals: (Use Bankrate.com to find information on how to pay off loans early and see ammoritization schedules, etc.)
Add $5,000 to Savings Account by June 2013

Investments:	Current Balance
Current Stocks / Bonds Value:	$1,000.00
Savings Account Balance:	$5,000.00
College Account Balance:	$25,000.00
Total Investments:	$31,000.00

Goals / Bucket List of things I want to do...
Graduate college
Travel
$50,000 in bank by 30 years old

Preparing for College

Preparing for college and choosing which college to attend can be very stressful for everyone involved. Keeping college information organized and easily accessible can make this process a lot less complicated. It is essential to find or purchase a file box to store and organize college information, pamphlets, and mailings as soon as possible. Make sure you start this file box early (before it's time to start applying to any colleges).

For the files inside the file box, try choosing a set of files with different colors (three or more is best). Then separate these files into categories (one category per color). Categories may include:

1) Colleges

   a) Sort by name of college, listing the first choice in the front of the file box and the last choice towards the back of the file box.

2) Funding and scholarships

   a) Sort by name of funding source or scholarship, in alphabetical order.

3) SAT, Test Scores, Grades.

   a) Sort by name of test taken or school attended where grades were given.

Once a college has been chosen and the student has been accepted, the file box can then hold the information for the particular college that was chosen. Again, start by categorizing the information.

Such categories can include:

1)   Health records.

2)   Job opportunities to pay for college.

3)   College loan information.

4)   Current financial plan.

5)   What to bring and shopping list.

6)   Paperwork needed for college.

7)   Do before leaving for college.

If all college information is kept in this one file box then everyone involved will always know where to look for any information needed.

Leaving for College

When any student is preparing to leave for college, it can be extremely helpful to have a list to help them prepare ahead of time: A "Do Before Leaving for College" list and a "What to Bring to College" list.

Most dorm rooms now come with a bed, desk, chair, closet, and dresser and not much else. Check with your college to see what the rules and regulations are, or if there are any special sizes of any of the items you may need to bring with you, such as needing extra-long sheets to fit the bed or having a limit on the size of microwave or refrigerator you can purchase.

Shop ahead of time so you will have plenty of time to prepare and find good deals that will save you money. Be sure to check with any possible future roommates to see what they are bringing so you do not end up with two of the same items that are not needed.

Do Before Leaving for College

1) Visit your college and get as much information as possible. Ask about safety, costs and financial aid, schedules, books, where to purchase items, where to get help, school personnel, etc.

2) Secure funding.

3) Create a budget.

4) Make sure all finances are accessible.

5) Set up class schedule.

6) Purchase books needed for classes.

7) Purchase meal plan.

8) Contact your roommate.

9) Shop for any needed items.

10) If necessary, visit the doctor and dentist for a check-up.

11) Transfer any prescriptions to a pharmacy near the college

12) Pack.

13) Create a contact list to bring with you.

14) Find ways to avoid interruptions to study time and learn how to manage your time.

What to Bring to College

1) Food Items

   a) Microwave safe plates and bowls.

   b) Glasses, cups, coffee mugs, travel mug, water bottle.

   c) Utensils.

   d) Snack bag clips, food storage containers.

   e) Can and bottle opener.

   f) Coffee maker.

   g) Small refrigerator.

   h) Microwave (check with your college to see rules and regulations for appliances).

   i) Food to snack on.

2) For the Bed

   a) Two sets of bed sheets (check with your college to see what size you will need, most likely extra-long twin).

   b) Comforter, blankets.

   c) Pillows.

   d) Pillow cases.

   e) Mattress pad or cover.

   f) Bedside caddy.

   g) Bed lifts.

    h) Alarm clock.

3) Dorm Room Items

    a) Dry erase board with markers or bulletin board with pushpins.

    b) Surge protectors.

    c) Lamp.

    d) Fan.

    e) Desk.

    f) Bookcase.

    g) Chair.

    h) Laptop accessories, lock for laptop.

    i) Mirror (full-length and handheld).

    j) Noise cancelling headphones or earplugs.

    k) Area rug.

4) Laundry

    a) Hamper.

    b) Laundry detergent, fabric softener, stain remover.

    c) Drying rack.

    d) Hangers.

    e) Iron, ironing board.

5) Cleaning

    a) Handheld vacuum.

b) Small broom and dustpan.

c) Waste basket, garbage bags.

d) Room deodorizer.

e) Air purifier.

f) Toilet brush, toilet cleaner.

g) All-purpose cleaner.

h) Dish drainer, dish soap.

i) Paper towels.

j) Lint roller.

k) Cleaning sponges.

6) What to Wear

a) Bathrobe, slippers, pajamas.

b) Sweatshirts, t-shirts, pants, shorts, socks, underwear.

c) Sportswear, swimsuit, workout clothes.

d) Sneakers, shoes, boots, sandals.

e) Raincoat, winter coat, hats, gloves, scarf.

7) Storage

a) Under the bed storage.

b) Plastic containers (small and large).

c) Organizers for the desk, drawers, closet, shoes, etc.

d) Hooks.

    e) Luggage.

8) Personal Hygiene

    a) Towels, wash cloths, hand towels.

    b) Shower caddy, soap holder, toothbrush holder and cover, shower shoes.

    c) Hair dryer, curling iron or straightener, hair spray, gel, hair ties.

    d) Toothbrush, toothpaste, mouthwash, shampoo, conditioner, shavers, body soap, Q-tips.

    e) Nail clippers, nail file, lotion, cosmetics.

    f) Tissues, toilet paper.

9) Study Supplies

    a) Paper, notebooks.

    b) Paperclips, binder clips.

    c) Tape.

    d) Scissors.

    e) Post-its.

    f) Post-it tabs or page markers.

    g) Stapler, staples.

    h) White-out.

    i) Index cards.

    j) Stamps, envelopes.

k) Folders.

l) Binders.

m) Highlighters, markers, pens, pencils, pencil sharpener.

n) Calculator or scientific calculator.

o) Book light.

p) Audio recorder.

q) USB flash drive or memory stick.

r) Laptop, laptop carrying case, wireless mouse, laptop cooling station.

s) Printer, ink, printer paper.

t) Paper shredder.

u) Backpack.

10) Miscellaneous

a) Light bulbs.

b) Batteries.

c) Flashlight.

d) Duct tape.

e) Extension cords.

f) Adapters.

g) Chargers.

h) Cell phone.

i) Contact list.

j) GPS.

k) Tool kit.

l) First aid kit.

m) Sewing kit.

n) Medications (prescription and over the counter), pill sorter, vitamins.

o) Sunblock, bug spray.

p) Gum.

q) Lockable file cabinet or lockbox.

r) Digital camera.

s) Music with music playing device.

t) TV with remote, TV stand.

u) DVD player.

v) Dorm décor.

w) Umbrella.

x) Contact, contact solutions, glasses.

Chapter Sixteen

In The Closet

There are many different closet organizers on the market these days, too many to mention here. Do your research online and visit several home improvement stores to get some ideas. Always be sure to measure and plan the layout of your closet before making any purchases.

Separate Clothing

Use different colors or different style hangers in your closet to help separate and quickly find the clothing you are looking for. You can do this to separate clean clothes from any clothes that have been worn briefly but are not quite ready for the laundry. You can also do this to separate work clothes from casual wear. Get creative and use whatever method works best for you.

Briefly Worn Clothing

Store clothing that has been worn briefly and you would like to wear again before washing in a separate section of the closet. If hung on a hanger, turn that one hanger backwards and leave the rest forward. If you use different color hangers or different style hangers, use only one specific color or style for those clothes that were worn briefly.

How to Organize a Closet and Quickly Determine Which Clothes to Get Rid Of

Figuring out which clothes to toss and which to keep can sometimes be a challenge. Try storing clothes you do not use often towards the back of the closet by placing each one of your recently worn items towards the front of the closet each time you put them away. You will soon find that the clothes you never seem to wear will end up in the very back of the closet. When you try to decide which clothes to get rid of to help make room for new ones, start in this area of the closet.

Chapter Seventeen

Gardening

Springtime Planting

If you like to garden, find a basket that's easy to carry to store your gardening supplies. A plastic one with a handle (usually used for holding cleaning products and found at most dollar stores) is a great choice because it is easy to clean. Or simply use any old basket you are no longer using for anything else. Just make sure the basket you choose is sturdy, easy to carry, and can hold everything you will need.

Use it to store:

1) Seeds.

2) Gardening tools.

3) Clipboard, pens, pencils, and paper (to help keep track of what you planted).

Use the basket for anything else you many need so it is all at your fingertips wherever you may need to use it.

If you collect seeds from your plants in the fall, try storing them in old spice containers or an old grated cheese container (one you have first thoroughly cleaned, of course). These containers also make wonderful seed dispensers come springtime, and this is a great way to recycle.

Garden Layout

When preparing a garden it can be extremely beneficial to plan where each plant will be placed before it is planted.

You can simply draw the shape of each planting bed (by hand or with the help of a computer program such as Microsoft Paint) and write or type in each item you wish to plant in each one.

Make sure to get a recommended measurement between plants and beds ahead of time so you will know just how many of each item can be planted.

Planning your garden out ahead of time can prevent a lot of hassle and reduce waste if you figure out just what you will need prior to purchasing your plants and seeds.

Plant Progress

To track the progress of each plant, try using a program such as Microsoft Excel.

Suggestions for categories:

1) Name of plants or seeds.

2) Date they were planted.

3) Where they were planted (if garden beds were used, which one).

4) How many were planted.

5) What fertilizers were used.

6) When to expect germination.

7) When the plant actually germinated.

8) When you harvested (for fruits and vegetables).

9) When you saw the first bloom (for flowers).

10) Overall results.

11) Ideas for next year.

The more information you keep track of, the more informed your decisions will be for the next garden. This will result in a better garden each year.

Chapter Eighteen

Shopping

All family members should be able to add to the family shopping list and this list should always be available to the one who actually does the shopping.

There are many different ways to create and use a shopping list. You can store it in your cell phone, on your computer, or simply write it down.

For those who save their shopping lists on their cell phones to share with others (yes, there is an app for that too), simply add items when needed. For those who do not shop and do not have access to the list but want to add to it, have them write down what they need for the person who *does* have access to the list.

For others who like to keep their shopping lists on paper or stored in a file on their computer, simply update and add as necessary, then (if saved on the computer) print out an updated copy whenever it's needed.

If you have a list with all the usual items you need but do not currently need them all, simply print out your list and have family members circle or highlight what you will need right away.

Extra Long Shopping Lists

If you frequently have a long list of items and still want to make your next shopping trip quick and easy while remembering everything you need, try creating two separate categories on your list.

You can separate these categories on two different pieces of paper, or simply separate each section on one sheet of paper by listing them at the top or bottom, or left and right side, depending on how long your list is.

Then separate those categories into subcategories and list by the layout of the store where you shop most often.

Example:

1) *Category 1*: Food and grocery store items (for any food items usually found at the grocery store).

   a) Produce.

   b) Breakfast items.

   c) Canned items.

   d) Baking supplies.

   e) Drinks.

   f) Meats, fish, and poultry.

   g) Refrigerated items.

h) Frozen items.

i) Miscellaneous.

2) *Category 2*: Supplies and other store items (for any items you need and will find at stores other than the grocery store).

a) Personal hygiene.

b) Medications.

c) Paper products.

d) Pet supplies.

e) Cleaning supplies.

f) Outdoor supplies.

g) Seasonal.

h) Kitchen.

i) Office.

j) Bedroom.

k) Bathroom.

l) Family members.

m) Miscellaneous.

Highlight or bold any items that are needed immediately and add in notes of what stores to shop at, sale prices, and any wish list items. Listing wish list items is helpful and can be a great timesaver when trying to think of gift ideas.

Keep this shopping list somewhere in your kitchen (hung up on the refrigerator, in a kitchen drawer, or inside a cabinet door) and be sure to always have a pen or pencil right next to it. Make it a family rule that if you take the last of something, you will be the one responsible for writing that item on the list so it can be replaced.

Sales and Coupons

The easiest way to organize your coupons is to simply purchase a coupon organizer that separates your coupons by category. If you do not want to purchase a coupon organizer, try using any of the following items depending on how many coupons you have and how you want to use your coupon organizer:

1) Large envelope.

2) Binder with transparent inserts.

3) Small container: separate coupons into categories using labeled index cards.

Go through your coupons monthly to find and dispose of any that have expired.

If you have coupons for any items on your lists make a note next to the item.

Example:

1) Milk

2) Cheese (cpn)

3) Butter

4) Bread (cpn)

This will remind you to use your coupon when you are at the store.

If you check sale flyers before shopping and shop at several stores to help achieve the best prices, make a note next to each item that is on sale. Write the name of the store (abbreviated) and sale price next to it.

Example:

1) Milk (PC $2.99 gal.)

2) Cheese

3) Butter (WM $1.99 ea.)

4) Bread

If you bring coupons with you, separate them into the same categories as your shopping list for quicker and easier reference and place the ones you intend to use that day to the front of each section or in the front of the coupon organizer under a separate section labeled "use next trip."

Planning ahead will allow you to save the most time and money on any shopping trip.

Organize Your Life and More ~ Christina Scalise

Sample shopping list

	Food / Grocery Store Items
Produce:	apples / lettuce / berries / brussel sprouts / cabbage / celery / pears /
Breakfast:	shredded wheat / oatmeal (cpn.) / kid's cereal / breakfast bars / bagels
Canned items:	corn / mushrooms / tomato sauce & paste / black olives / beets / TUNA / soup
Baking supplies:	olive oil / white vinegar /oregano
Drinks:	orange juice / apple juice / milk ($2.99 / gal. @ PC, cpn.) / ice-tea /
Meats/Fish/Poultry:	fish /ground beef / chicken /
Refrigerated items:	cheese / yogurt ($.65 ea @ PC)
Frozen items:	pizza / bacon / french fries / ice-cream / butter (cpn.)
Miscellaneous:	pickles / pasta / frosting / sour cream
	Supplies / Other Store Items
Personal hygiene:	razors / deodorant / toothpaste / shampoo & conditioner
Medications:	allergy medicine / bandaides /
Paper Products:	small box tissues for work & home / reg. size tissues for home / paper plates / paper towels / toilet paper
Pet supplies:	dog food (weight control formula)
Cleaning supplies:	dishwasher detergent / laundry detergent / dryer sheets / small vacuum
Outdoor supplies:	work gloves / outdoor thermometer /
Seasonal:	Christmas dinnerware
Kitchen:	electric can opener
Office:	small notepads / copy paper / ink --- [OFFICE SUPPLY STORE – is having a sale this week]
Bedroom:	king size bed sheets/
Bathrooms:	towels
Mom:	pants / watch / winter hat & gloves
Dad:	jeans
Son:	backpack for school / winter coat --- [video game for birthday is on sale at department store this week]
Daughter:	sweatshirts
Miscellaneous:	AA batteries / instant glue

Chapter Nineteen

Food

Recipes

Most of us have a collection of family recipes we like to use and some we would like to try. Getting those recipes organized can be a challenge. Try creating your own family recipe book. Take an ordinary binder and add page protectors for full page recipes and photo album inserts that will fit other size recipes. These will help protect the recipes from splattered ingredients and are a great way to hold your recipes in place. Another way to add recipes to your binder is to use ordinary loose leaf paper so you can tape the recipes to the papers inside the binder.

Use whatever works to keep those recipes in place.

You can also insert dividers to separate your recipes into categories. Some category suggestions are: Appetizers and Snacks, Beverages, Breads, Cakes and Frostings, Candy and Ice Cream, Cookies, Desserts, Eggs, Cheese, Legumes and Casseroles, Fish and Shellfish, Freezing and Canning, Meat and Lasagnas, Pasta,

Rice and Grains, Pies and Pizza, Poultry and Chicken Entrees, Salads and Dressings, Sauces, Relishes, Salsas and Dips, Soups, Stews and Stir Fry, Vegetables, Special Helps, and Miscellaneous. Binders can be very useful because they can easily be updated by adding or removing recipes at any time.

It also helps to write comments on or next to the recipes you have tried (who liked them and how good it was on a scale of 1—10). Toss out those recipes no one liked; why keep them? Try to set aside one night each week to try a new recipe and see how fast you go through those recipes you've always wanted to try. After you have tried each new recipe, immediately choose another recipe to try; that way you will have time to shop for the ingredients before you try out the next one the following week.

Restaurant Takeout Menus

Do you have a lot of takeout menus scattered around your home, or maybe stuffed in a drawer somewhere? If you only have a few of them, try storing them in a pocket folder to help keep them in order. If you have too many to fit into a folder, store them in alphabetical order in a binder instead, using pocket dividers to hold each one. After you have done this, you will find it is a lot easier to quickly find the one you need. Keep them updated by replacing older menus with newer ones regularly.

"Grab and Go" Snacks

These days, everyone is so busy it's hard to make time to stop and get something nutritious to eat. We often find ourselves on the run, getting unhealthy takeout food or grabbing prepackaged junk food. It's nice to finally see more and more healthy choices at the grocery stores and at fast food places, but when you find that you or your family members are constantly running out of the house without having something healthy to eat, it may be time to consider having a snack box ready to go at all times.

For the refrigerator: Have a healthy snack area, container, or drawer set aside strictly for grab-and-go items. Suggestions for these items and other quick healthy snacks are bite-size fruits and vegetables ready to go in snack bags or in a bowl that is easy to reach into and grab what you want. Bite size snacks can include:

1) Vegetables: celery, carrots (peeled), cauliflower, broccoli, etc.

2) Fruits: apples (or apples slices), plums, pears, peaches, grapes, orange slices, etc.

3) Other items: Single-size yogurts (yogurt in tubes), cheese sticks, nutritional drinks, bagels or pre-made breakfast sandwiches (bagels with cheese, eggs, bacon, sausage, etc.).

In the pantry: Have one open container or box (shoebox size is great) filled with grab and go items such as:

1) Prepackaged items: crackers (those filled with cheese, peanut butter and jelly, etc. tend to be more filling), beef jerky or beef sticks, small boxes of raisins, applesauce singles and pudding cups (include a plastic spoon), pretzels, chips, breakfast bars, etc.

2) Small snack bags filled with: cereal, crackers, dried fruit, nuts, trail mix, pudding cups, rice cakes, popcorn, pretzels, chips, etc.

Organize Your Life and More ~ Christina Scalise

In the car: Any food that will last through extreme temperatures, such as dry crackers in a sealed bag.

Place all items together in one container so there are many choices in plain view to quickly choose from and grab on the go.

Make it a point to refill these containers and areas with ready-to-go snacks once a week, or after each shopping trip as you put away your groceries. Having these grab-and-go items available daily will help keep you and your family fed and help to avoid choosing those unhealthy last-minute alternatives.

Cook in Bulk and Freeze to Save Time and Effort

When making any meal or snack, consider making extra. Double or triple the recipe and make as many as you can every time you cook or bake, then freeze what you will not be using that day.

Several items that freeze well, just to name a few:

1) Breakfast sandwiches.

2) Pancakes, waffles.

3) Pasta sauce.

4) Meatballs.

5) Burgers.

6) Pies.

7) Desserts (including cookie dough).

8) Casseroles.

9) Lasagna.

10) Stews and soups.

11) Stuffed peppers.

12) Pizza.

13) Bread.

14) Meatloaf.

15) Chili.

Wrap or place each one in a sealed container or freezer bag, then date and freeze for another day. Doing this will give you more options when looking for a quick, easy meal or snack.

Remember to Take Your Dinner Out of the Freezer the Night Before

There are several ways to remind yourself and your family to take dinner out of the freezer the night before. The trick is finding the solution that fits your family best.

Here are a few ideas:

1) Keep an erasable board next to the refrigerator. This can also be a great place for your family to write down some dinner ideas for the week.

2) Post-it note on the refrigerator, mirror, or anywhere else you will be looking before going to bed.

3) Choose one token item to serve as a simple reminder to take dinner out of the freezer, and place it in a spot where you will be sure to see it. Always use the same token item every time so you will remember what it is reminding you to do. You can choose something as

simple as a small decorative figure or even a plant, anything that will catch your eye if it is out of place. Once you have remembered to take dinner out, simply place the item back where it belongs. Hint: If you are afraid you will forget what the token is reminding you to do, simply place a note, or write a note in permanent marker, on the bottom of the item.

4) Start discussing and planning your next meal every night during dinner. Make sure to write down ideas so you can shop and plan ahead, and take the time to take out anything that needs to be thawed while you are cleaning up from that night's meal.

If one reminder doesn't work for you and your family, simply try another way until you find something that will work when needed.

Keep Your Food Fresh

Keeping your food fresh in the pantry, refrigerator, freezer, and anywhere else you store food isn't difficult if you consistently place new items in the same area.

After any shopping trip, pull older items forward and place newer ones in the back so the oldest ones will be used first. If you do not want to pull the older items forward, try consistently pushing them to the left or right, or up or down to the next shelf; the key is to be consistent with how you do it.

For refrigerator items, pay attention to expiration dates and try not keep any leftovers more than a week (for some foods, less than one week may be necessary).

Be sure to mark an expiration date or the date you purchased the item if it does not already have an expiration date on it. Again, the key here is to be consistent with how you do it.

Chapter Twenty

Projects

Organizing Project Parts and Information

Having several projects going at once is common for most individuals and families. Keeping the paperwork together, organized, and handy for each of those projects can be a challenge.

For projects with a moderate amount of paperwork, a simple file will do. Whether it's looking into new insurance rates, researching the best value for an upcoming purchase, or a simple remodeling project, keeping your papers in order will help the project go smoothly. Any time you start a new project, start a new file and label each file with the name of your project. (Example: "Garage Remodeling Project.") If you have small parts that need to be kept with the file, place them in an envelope to put into the file with the paperwork. If you have larger items that need to go with the paperwork, keep those items stored next to the file cabinet or box where your paperwork is being stored. Ongoing project files should be kept together in a file cabinet or box for easy access.

For larger projects with a lot of paperwork involved, such as planning a wedding, building a new home, or a new business idea, binders may be a better choice. For these projects use binders with page protectors and dividers to help separate each category of paperwork. Using dividers with pockets will also give you more storage room and can be very useful. If a binder isn't large enough to hold it all, you may want to invest in a file box for your project.

Keeping your paperwork organized for each project will give you quick and easy access to all important, needed information, saving you lots of time and stress while working on the project. The more informed you are throughout your project, the smoother it will go and the better results you will have in the end.

Grab and Go Fix-It Bag

Keep essential tools ready to go in a small bag or a carry-all container. In the bag, you can place hammers, screwdrivers, pliers, tape measure, and anything else you may need to have handy for any household repairs.

Chapter Twenty-One

Organizing Specific Items

Medications

Medicine cabinets can become messy very quickly, which can result in frustration when trying to find what you need. To organize your medicine cabinet, start by emptying the entire cabinet and spreading everything out so you can get a good look at what you have. Pull out expired items and those you no longer intend to use and get rid of them immediately. Organize the rest into categories such as cold medications, pain relievers, antacids, and vitamins and place them into baskets or small containers that will be easy to grab in a hurry. To help you find the correct prescription quickly each day, mark prescriptions (using permanent marker or small stickers on the cap) with the purpose of the prescription (pain, cholesterol, allergies, etc.).

If your family members each have a lot of prescriptions, medications, and vitamins set aside just for them, choose a small container or basket for each individual to store their items. And always remember to store your medications in a safe place, out of the reach of small children.

For those who have trouble remembering to take their pills, weekly and daily dispensers are a great idea. If a dispenser is not desired, try using a calendar to mark each day that you have taken your medication. A simple check mark will do each time you take your medication; then if you have forgotten whether you have taken it or not, all you have to do is look at the calendar to see if that day was marked.

If you have to take a certain medication every few hours, keep a written schedule of the times you have taken each dosage and when the next dosage will be due. Set a timer if necessary. There are several gadgets on the market now to help remind you when to take your medication. You can also simply set the alarm on your cell phone or watch as a reminder.

For doctors' appointments, be sure to bring a list of all prescription medications, vitamins, and supplements you are currently taking, what the dosage amount is, and how often you take each item. Write down all side effects and reactions you experience with each medication as well.

Keys

Keep keys in a decorative basket or bowl or hang them on a key hanger. Label each set of keys with a clip-on key tag or give each key a different color. You can purchase clip-on key tags at most office supply stores. *Make sure to have those spares hidden away for those days when you lock yourself out.*

Pet Toys

Place pet toys in a large decorative basket or box on the floor for your pets. This is a great way to store these items and still make them accessible to the pets who use them.

Creative Storage for Kitchen Utensils

If you have too many kitchen utensils and not enough storage space, it may be time to get creative.

Find any large, decorative item, make sure it has been sanitized, and then place your utensils (in an upright position) inside the container you have chosen and place it on your countertop. Make sure the item you choose will be heavy and steady enough to work with so it will not fall over every time you reach for a utensil.

Here are a few items you may find useful for holding your kitchen utensils (large and small):

1) Oversized jar

2) Plant pot

3) Vase

4) Old crock pot

5) Pitcher

6) Extra-large coffee mug

7) Extra-large pencil cup

Paint, Paint Supplies, and Paint Samples

Painting can create a stockpile of supplies. Paint cans, brushes, stirring sticks, paint samples, and so much more can quickly litter your garage and cellar.

For Paint Cans: Label each paint can (using permanent marker) with the name of the color (and color code if applicable), rooms painted, and the date you purchased the paint.

Store paint in airtight containers. Do not let the paint freeze or leave it in an area where it will be exposed to extremely hot temperatures for long periods of time. Make sure the temperature is between 40°F and 90°F.

Paint Samples: If you kept a copy of the color sample, write down the date and which room you painted on the back of the sample.

If you keep a lot of paint samples on hand for possible future use, it may be time to sort through them and decide which ones can be thrown out and which ones can be kept.

Once you have decided on the ones you want to keep, divide the saved samples into three categories:

1) Colors currently used in the house.

2) Colors to use in the future.

3) All other color samples.

Place each category of samples into a large, labeled envelope.

If you want to take it a step further, divide them into subcategories separated by color and place them one behind the other in a small container, or simply clip the different categories of colors together inside the envelope.

Paint Supplies: New (unused) paint supplies such as brushes, stirring sticks, and rollers can be stored in an airtight container to keep them from collecting dust and dirt.

Extra Parts

We all have those extra parts that came with a new item that had to be installed or put together such as furniture, light fixtures, and equipment. Manufacturers tend to send extra parts with products so you will have them on hand in case one is broken or lost.

These extra parts can be placed separately in labeled Ziploc bags and placed one in front of the other in one large box, container, or file drawer.

Gift Bags and Wrapping

How to organize special occasion gift bags and wrappings:

For gift bags: Organize gift bags in a large container and sort them from smallest to largest. If you reuse them, remember to hang a tag on the outside of the gift bag saying who the gift bag originally came from, so when you reuse it you don't give it back to the same person. Be sure to separate the used from the new by placing used bags in a separate labeled container.

For wrapping paper: Start by throwing out wrapping paper that is too small or too damaged to use. Then place wrapping paper tubes in a container for storage. There are several types of storage containers to choose from. Vertical containers are nice because they take up less floor space, and long horizontal ones are nice for storing under a bed. Another option is to simply place them in the drawers of an old dresser.

Keep your rolls of paper from unraveling by placing rubber bands around them, or just place empty wrapping paper, paper towel, or toilet paper tubes (sliced open so they can easily expand) around each tube of paper. If they do not fit snugly enough around the roll of paper, add a rubber band around the tube to help hold them in place. This will help keep the paper in place and prevent damage. When using rubber bands on wrapping paper, make sure you don't wrap the rubber band too tightly or it will crease the paper.

For all other items: Store ribbons, bows, tape, pens, markers, tags, and other accessories in a small basket or container. Bows should always be on top or separated into their own container to prevent them from being flattened.

Ten Ways to Organize Those Smallest of Items

Do you have a large pile of small items somewhere in your home that you don't want to deal with? They might be made up of small items such as craft supplies, sewing supplies, jewelry, small office supplies, or leftover nuts, bolts, nails, and screws.

Organizing those piles can be simple if you use the correct item to sort them. You can either purchase an organizer or simply look around your home for something you already have on hand that may be useful.

Organize Your Life and More ~ Christina Scalise

Start by going through the pile and immediately discarding everything you no longer want or need. Then separate by category (size, color, or type of item). Once you have the pile separated into categories, you can then see how large your containers or organizer compartments need to be. Then it is time to find something that will fit that need.

Once you have found something that will work, the items can be categorized and sorted by size or type using any of the following containers:

1) Organizing bin with small labeled drawers.

2) Tackle boxes.

3) Tool boxes.

4) Drawer organizers.

5) Ice cube trays.

6) Silverware trays.

7) Egg cartons.

8) Extra small bowls.

9) Ring boxes.

10) Recycled clear plastic jars such as those used for:

    a) Spices.

    b) Peanut butter.

    c) Takeout food.

    d) Grated cheese.

Cosmetics, Nail Accessories, and Hair Accessories

Small items such as cosmetics, nail accessories, and hair accessories are much easier to find when neatly organized. If you simply toss them into a drawer or a cabinet, they can quickly pile up and become hard to find when needed.

Use cosmetic organizers, small containers, or baskets inside of drawers, in your cabinets, or on your countertops to help separate items.

Here are some ways to keep them organized:

First: Immediately toss what you no longer need or want.

Second: Separate cosmetics, nail accessories, and hair accessories.

Third: Separate as follows:

1) For cosmetics, separate into three categories:

   a) Used daily.

   b) Used once in a while.

   c) Backup supplies.

2) For nail accessories, separate into categories such as:

   a) Nail polish (sorted by color, if necessary).

   b) Nail polish remover.

   c) Nail files, clippers, trimmers, etc.

3) For hair accessories, separate into categories such as:

   a) Ties, clips, and bows.

b) Curling irons, straighteners, blow dryer.

c) Trimmers, scissors, etc.

d) Brushes, combs, hair pick.

e) Sprays and gels.

If you don't want to spend a lot of money organizing these items, look around your home and see what can be reused. You can use any small basket, container, bowl, or even an old tackle box. You don't have to spend a lot of money to get the job done.

Hobby Rooms

Hobby rooms should be a fun, relaxing place to escape from daily life and work on your hobbies. Here are some tips on how to make it that way:

Make it worker friendly. Set up lighting where you will need it the most, set up a radio or television to listen to while you work, hang nice inspirational pictures on the wall, etc.

Give yourself plenty of room to work. Have work tables available to use and plenty of counter space to lay out your projects.

Give yourself ample places to store your items. Use shelving, hooks to hang items on, cabinets, etc.

Separate your tools into categories and arrange by size. Either hang them up or neatly place them in a drawer.

Use clear and labeled storage containers. This way you can quickly find what you are looking for.

Decorate in a fun way that inspires you.

Once your hobby room has been organized, you should be able to relax without searching for anything and enjoy your hobby to its fullest.

Pictures

If you save pictures on your computer, create files and separate each file by category, and then date them. Don't forget to back up your files.

If you save them in a box, separate them by category or date using oversized index cards.

If you enjoy scrapbooking, getting your photos organized will help you find the photos you are looking for quickly and easily.

Movies, DVDs, Music, and CDs

The best way to organize these items is to store them in a vertical position. If you stack them one on top of the other, it can be very difficult to quickly grab the one you want to use. Get rid of the ones you no longer enjoy and simply organize the rest by genre or in alphabetical order.

Taming Your Cords and Wires

Label cords behind your desk, television, etc. with tape, tabs, or small clips.

1) Start by identifying each one.

2) Get rid of any that are not needed.

3) Label each remaining one. Use different colored labels or markers for quicker identification.

4) Bundle longer wires using Velcro straps, rubber bands, zip ties or twist ties.

5) Hang as many wires as possible out of the way (use Command strips or hooks to do this).

Replace That Rolodex

Save your contact information in an easy-to-update Excel file instead of a Rolodex. Storing your contact information on your computer will allow you to easily update it when necessary. If you prefer to have a hard copy available at all times, simply print one out when needed. Once a year, update your list by deleting contacts you no longer need, and always back up your file.

Selling Your Home

Organization and reducing clutter is very important when trying to sell your home. The more organized your home is, the better it will look to potential buyers.

Start by getting rid of clutter. Throw away and store as much as you possibly can. File paperwork away and clean everything!

Store personal items. This includes pictures, personal collections, personal décor, etc. This will help the prospective buyer picture themselves in the home.

Reduce unnecessary furniture wherever possible. Less furniture gives the illusion of a larger room.

Make sure everything is in working order. Fix everything that needs repair such as:

1) Squeaky doors, cabinets, floors, etc.

2) Cracks in sidewalks.

3) Holes in siding, floors, walls.

4) Leaky faucets, toilets, pipes.

5) Make sure lights and light switches are in working order, and replace any blown light bulbs.

Apply fresh paint wherever necessary. A newly painted room not only gives it a fresh new look, but can also make a room look larger if you use a lighter color. Neutral colors work best when trying to appeal to potential buyers.

Let in the light. Turn on all lights inside your home and open windows and blinds to let in as much natural light as possible, unless there is something outside your window that is not an attractive sight.

Give your home an appealing smell. Add a fresh-smelling bouquet of flowers to your kitchen table or countertop, or simply plug in deodorizers, make a pot of coffee, or bake some cookies or a pie. Use anything to give your home a fresh, appealing smell for when your prospective buyers are touring your home.

Make a great first impression: Your home's first impression should always be at its best, including curb appeal and the entrance to the home. Start at the end of your driveway and take a walk through your front door; try to see your home through a potential buyer's eyes. What sticks out the most? Is it something that needs repair, cleaning, or maintenance? Are there any unappealing colors or objects? If so, remove and change whatever necessary.

Provide Details: Provide your realtor and potential buyers with a list of details about your home. Include up-to-date pictures of the best areas in your home, financial information, repair dates, and any other information that may be of use or interesting to potential buyers.

A little organization, cleaning, and prep work can make all the difference in a potential buyer making the decision to purchase your home or walk away.

Garage

When organizing your garage, first start by determining what you would like to use the garage for. Do you need to park your car in it? Do you want it strictly for storage use? Will it be used as an additional recreation area?

Once you have made that decision, get rid of everything that is broken or no longer needed. Then you will need to take out everything that will no longer be used inside the garage area and store it somewhere else in your home.

Next, group the remaining items into categories and designate an area for each category. You may want to organize by function or season.

Examples:

1) Tools and project area. Workbenches with pegboards are especially helpful when organizing tools and creating an area to work on your projects.

179

2) Gardening and lawn maintenance area.

3) Winter outdoor equipment.

4) Summer outdoor equipment.

5) Sports equipment.

6) Car maintenance area.

There are many different organizers on the market to help you organize your gardening, outdoor, and sports equipment, as well as many other items and areas of your garage. Before you spend money on these products, take a good look at what you have that needs to be organized. Then you can choose the correct organizer, or simply try to organize the best you can by using what you already have on hand. You may be surprised to learn that all you need are a few shelves, hooks, and properly labeled storage boxes, or you may decide that the one organizer you've had your eye on for a while will fit your needs perfectly.

When organizing your garage it is important to get as much as you can off the floor. Install shelving and hooks, and don't forget you can also use the ceiling and the area above the ceiling to store items as well. Get creative and find those hidden storage areas that will serve you well.

Chapter Twenty-Two

Recycle and Reuse

Y̶ou can recycle containers and reuse baskets, bookshelves, boxes, and many other items around the house. Whether you choose to spend money on organizing products or recycle what you already have on hand, organizing your household can be done easily if you use the right item.

Recycle Those Unused Containers

Container storage is a great way to keep organized. Clear containers are usually the best choice, but other items that can be used include unused vases, coffee mugs, and containers your everyday products come in such as spices, peanut butter, deli items, and grated cheese, along with takeout containers and popcorn tins. Even cat litter containers can be reused. Just make sure you thoroughly wash out each container before reusing them.

Hint: The smaller containers are great for storing small office supplies, buttons, and more. And containers with pop-up tops on them, such as spice containers and grated cheese containers, work great for storing and dispensing nails, push pins, screws, and seeds for planting.

Storage Containers

Keeping a small stockpile of recycled containers on hand can help you organize just about anything whenever you have the time and are thinking about it.

A good place to store these extra containers is in one clear, extra-large container. To help yourself limit the amount you keep, make it a rule to only allow yourself one large container worth of space for storing these items. Or set aside one small area for those containers. Once you start running out of room, start throwing out the least desirable ones or some of the ones you have too many of. The important thing to remember is not to keep too many, because it will create unnecessary clutter.

Some items you may consider keeping: plastic containers, zippered bags, small boxes, jars; basically anything that can be reused to hold small items.

Add in a few small drawer organizers, containers, or baskets you may have picked up from your local store or dollar shop to keep on hand as well. These are very inexpensive and you will be surprised at how often you will use them in drawers, cabinets, etc.

Keeping these small items on hand and ready for use will help you recycle, save money, and quickly organize many different areas of your home whenever you have the time to do so.

Baskets

Do you have empty baskets around your home that are decorative but have no real purpose? Baskets are great organizational tools and can be both decorative and useful.

Baskets used for storage can hold many different items such as:

1) Linens.

2) Children's toys.

3) Pet toys.

4) Jewelry.

5) Books.

6) In the office: keys, office supplies, notecards.

7) In the kitchen: silverware, napkins, condiments, fruit, tea bags, grab-and-go items.

8) In the bathroom: towels, washcloths, toilet paper.

9) In a hobby room: knitting, string, yarn, other small supplies.

10) Anywhere: Miscellaneous catchall bin.

Baskets can also be useful when carrying items such as cleaning supplies, clothing, or several items at once, from room to room inside the home. They can also help in carrying items for outside projects to and from your house, shed, or garden. Use them to carry tools, supplies, fruits, vegetables, flowers, and so much more.

Besides organizing and carrying items, baskets can also be used for decorative purposes holding potpourri, pinecones, flowers, etc. Baskets can even be used as a small dog or cat bed. Of all the pet beds we have purchased over the years, a small basket has been our family cat's favorite place to sleep.

Binders

Binders are a great way to organize many different projects, recipes, photos, card collections, and much more. Organize your binders by category, date, or project, and label each section.

What Can You Recycle?

You would be surprised at how many different items you can reuse if you just use your imagination. Here are just a few ideas of recycled items and imagination gone wild:

Tackle boxes can hold:

1) Small hardware or tools.

2) Craft items.

3) Jewelry.

4) Makeup.

5) Office supplies.

6) Crayons, markers, pens, pencils, erasers.

7) Small collections.

   a) Toys.

   b) Rocks.

Dressers can hold:

1) Gift wrapping supplies: paper, bows, bags, etc.

2) Craft supplies.

3) Gloves, hats, scarves, etc.

4) Household supplies such as:

    a) Batteries.

    b) Light bulbs.

    c) Extension cords.

    d) Toolkit.

    e) String, rope.

5) Or remove drawers and replace with shelves.

Bookshelves can hold:

1) CDs, DVDs, Movies.

2) Paint cans.

3) Tools.

4) Gardening supplies.

5) Collections and décor.

6) Plants.

7) Or make a dollhouse out of it.

Ladders can hold:

1) Plants.

2) Hanging pots and pans.

3) Or use it to help your pets or other animals reach higher ground.

Plastic cups, coffee mugs, and glasses can hold:

1) Pens, pencils, markers.

2) Scissors.

3) Rulers.

4) Small office supplies, such as paperclips, erasers, rubber bands, and tacks.

5) Small hardware and tools.

6) Miscellaneous catchall.

7) Loose change holder.

8) Toothbrushes and toothpaste.

9) Cosmetics.

10) Kitchenware (spatulas, serving spoons, etc.).

11) Plants.

12) Anything you would like to scoop up and dispense (pet food, bird seed, etc.).

Chapter Twenty-Three

Organizing Challenges

Challenging yourself to organize certain areas of your life and home can give you the motivation to get it all done. It will also help you tackle each area one at a time so you do not feel overwhelmed by everything that needs to be done. Creating a list of these challenges will also help you remind yourself of your organizing goals.

The One-Week Challenge

Choose a week and set aside enough time every day to do some organizing. Choose seven things that need to be organized (one for each day of the week) and set aside enough time each day to fit the organizing project into your schedule. It can be something as small as organizing a drawer or cabinet to something as big as organizing an entire room in your home.

When the week is over and the projects have been completed, make sure to explain the new organization system to any family members, if necessary. Then take the time to enjoy what you have accomplished by rewarding yourself.

Challenges to Do

Listed on the next few pages are many different organizing challenges. It's up to YOU to choose which challenges you would like to accept and accomplish.

For the ones that do not apply to you or have already been done, simply place an "X" next to the challenge and then work on the rest.

Along with each challenge are chapter references to specific information that will help you complete each one. Try to do at least one organizing challenge every day, week, or month, depending on your own personal goals. Choose a day to do it, add it to your To Do list, schedule it in; do whatever you have to do to get it done.

There is also a page where you can fill in your own challenges. Fill that page with your own organizing goals.

To help keep track of the ones you have done already, simply mark off each challenge you have finished. When you are done, take time to enjoy the rewards of being organized.

Organizing Challenge

* Choose an item you are always losing and designate a place for it.

Chapter 2: "A Place for Everything and Everything in Its Place"

Chapter 9: "I Can't Remember Where I Put It!"

Organizing Challenge

* Choose an area that is cluttered with unused items and toss what is no longer wanted or needed.

Chapter 2: "Sometimes You Need to Make a Bigger Mess to Achieve Less Mess"

Organizing Challenge

* Create a Life Goals list

Chapter 3: The "To Do" List

Organizing Challenge

* Offer to help someone get organized in exchange for their help with one of your organizing projects.

Chapter 4: "Help Each Other"

Organizing Challenge

* Create a chore sheet for your children.

Chapter 2: "Using Spreadsheets to Organize Your Information"

Chapter 3: "Focus on Areas of the Greatest Concern"

Chapter 4: "How to Get Your Kids to Help With Household Chores"

Chapter 14: "Post Important Information Where It Is Needed Most"

Chapter 15: "Kids Need to Be Organized Too! This Includes Schedules, Chores, and Rules."

Chapter 15: "Chore Sheets"

Chapter 15: "Back to School"

Organizing Challenge

* Find something to organize vertically to save space.

Chapter 6: "Keep It Stored Vertically"

Chapter 6: "Stack and Store Vertically or Horizontally to Save Room"

Chapter 6: "Empty Containers and Lids"

Chapter 7: "Wasted Spaces"

Chapter 21: "Movies, DVDs, Music, and CDs"

Organizing Challenge

* Organize your empty food storage containers and lids.

Chapter 6: "Empty Containers and Lids"

Organizing Challenge

* Find some wasted space in your home and create a storage area for some misplaced items.

Chapter 7: "Creative Storage"

Chapter 7: "Wasted Spaces"

Chapter 7: "Hidden Storage Hiding in Your Cabinets"

Organizing Challenge

* Designate a drawer, shelf, cabinet, or reachable storage area for your child's items.

Chapter 7: "Store Regularly Used Items Within Reach of Children"

Organizing Challenge

* Go through one or more boxes of items that have been in storage for a long time and get rid of as many items as possible.

Chapter 8: "I Have Too Much Stuff!"

Organizing Challenge

* Find an area in your home where you can regularly store unwanted items (examples of piles to create in this area: garage sale, charity, sell, bring to dump).

Chapter 2: "Sometimes Less Really is More"

Chapter 8: "Get Rid of Pile"

Organizing Challenge

* Place a "Discard Basket" in or near a family members' bedroom and encourage them to fill it up with unwanted items.

Chapter 8: "Discard Baskets"

Organizing Challenge

* Plan a garage sale.

Chapter 8: "How to Plan a Garage Sale"

Organizing Challenge

* Clean out and organize any junk drawer.

Chapter 8: "How to Organize a Junk Drawer"

Organizing Challenge

* Set up a bill paying system to help remind you when each bill is due.

Chapter 7: "Within Reach"

Chapter 9: "Remember to Pay Those Bills on Time"

Chapter 12: "Financial Layout"

Chapter 12: "Designate an Area for Bill Paying"

Chapter 13: "How to Keep up With Incoming Mail"

Organizing Challenge

* Create a family budget and lay out your family finances on paper, including all expenses.

Chapter 12: "Financial Layout"

Organizing Challenge

* Reevaluate your accounts to see if any can be eliminated.

Chapter 12: "Too Many Accounts"

Organizing Challenge

* Create a "Busy Bag" and fill it with everything you usually do not have time to deal with.

Chapter 2: "The ABC's of Organization"

Chapter 10: "Busy Bag"

Chapter 10: "Multitasking and Saving Time"

Organizing Challenge

* Tackle a pile of papers that has been sitting around for a while.

> **Chapter 8**: "General Rules to Controlling Clutter Before it Starts"

> **Chapter 13**: "Eight Ways to Reduce or Eliminate Those Piles of Papers"

> **Chapter 13**: "Questions to Ask Yourself Before Throwing Away Papers"

> **Chapter 13**: "Tackle That Drawer Full of Papers"

Organizing Challenge

* Go through your file cabinet and throw out any outdated files. Shred papers that may have personal or account information on them and simply toss the rest.

Organizing Challenge

* Organize your documents into folders on your computer.

> **Chapter 13**: "Computer Folders"

Organizing Challenge

* Set up a filing system for your receipts.

> **Chapter 12**: "Tax Receipts"

> **Chapter 13**: "Finding Your Receipts"

> **Chapter 13**: "Storage of Your Pending Receipts"

Organizing Challenge

* Create a family communication area somewhere in your home.

Chapter 14: "The Importance of Designating a Family Communication Area"

Chapter 14: "Post Important Information Where It Is Needed Most"

Organizing Challenge

* Challenge your child to get rid of ten items in less than ten minutes.

Chapter 3: "Pick a Number and Challenge Yourself"

Chapter 15: "Twenty Ways to Get Your Child to Pick up and Organize Their Bedroom—and Keep It That Way"

Organizing Challenge

* Create job cards, list available jobs for your kids, or post a Help Wanted sign.

Chapter 4: "Help Wanted"

Chapter 4: "How to Get Your Kids to Help With Household Chores"

Chapter 15: "Kids Need to Be Organized Too! This Includes Schedules, Chores and Rules."

Chapter 15: "Job Cards for Kids"

Chapter 15: "Rules Sheets"

Chapter 15: "Jobs List for Kids"

Organizing Challenge

* Create a rules sheet for your kids.

> **Chapter 2**: "Using Spreadsheets to Organize Your Information"

> **Chapter 15**: "Kids Need to Be Organized Too! This Includes Schedules, Chores and Rules."

> **Chapter 15**: "Rules Sheets"

> **Chapter 15**: "Leaving Your Children Home Alone"

Organizing Challenge

* Create a list of fun things for your kids to do.

> **Chapter 15**: "Have A "Fun Things to Do" List Ready To Go"

> **Chapter 15**: "Leaving Your Children Home Alone"

Organizing Challenge

* Help your kids plan for their future and college.

> **Chapter 15**: "Planning for the Future"

> **Chapter 15**: "Preparing for College"

> **Chapter 15**: "Leaving for College"

Organizing Challenge

* Go through your closet and get rid of any clothing and shoes you no longer wear.

> **Chapter 3**: "Pick a Number and Challenge Yourself"

> **Chapter 16**: "Separate Clothing"

Chapter 16: "How to Organize a Closet and Quickly Determine Which Clothes to Get Rid of"

Organizing Challenge

* Find an easy-to-carry basket or bucket and store your smaller gardening supplies in it.

Chapter 17: "Springtime Planting"

Organizing Challenge

* Go through your coupons and throw out any expired ones. Sort the rest into a coupon organizer.

Chapter 18: "Sales and Coupons"

Organizing Challenge

* Create a family recipe book and challenge your kids to do the same. While doing this, go through your pile of saved recipes and throw out the ones you know were not good and the ones you know you won't ever try. If saved on the computer, date and organize by category.

Chapter 4: "How to Get Your Kids to Help With Household Chores"

Chapter 19: "Recipes"

Chapter 22: "Binders"

Organizing Challenge

* Organize your restaurant takeout menus.

Chapter 19: "Restaurant Takeout Menus"

Organize Your Life and More ~ Christina Scalise

Organizing Challenge

* Set up a "Grab and Go" snack area in your pantry and refrigerator.

Chapter 10: "Individualize"

Chapter 19: "Grab and Go" Snacks

Chapter 19: "Cook in Bulk and Freeze to Save Time and Effort"

Organizing Challenge

* Clean out the pantry, refrigerator, and freezer, and throw out any expired items.

Chapter 19: "Keep Your Food Fresh"

Organizing Challenge

* Plan your next week's meals and add what you need to your grocery list.

Chapter 19: "Remember to Take Your Dinner Out of the Freezer the Night Before"

Organizing Challenge

* Organize any ongoing projects.

Chapter 20: "Project Organization"

Organizing Challenge

* Organize your medicine cabinet and throw out expired items.

Chapter 7: "Within Reach"

Chapter 14: "Post Important Information Where It Is Needed Most"

Chapter 21: "Medications"

Organizing Challenge

* Organize your paint supplies and throw out or recycle old brushes, rollers, and paint cans that are no longer usable.

Chapter 21: "Paint, Paint Supplies, and Paint Samples"

Organizing Challenge

* Organize your extra parts.

Chapter 20: "Project Organization"

Chapter 21: "Extra Parts"

Organizing Challenge

* Organize your gift bags and wrapping paper.

Chapter 21: "Gift Bags and Wrapping"

Chapter 22: "What Can You Recycle"

Organizing Challenge

* Organize your hardware (nails, screws, nuts, bolts, etc.).

Chapter 6: "Alphabetize or Sort By Size and Color"

Chapter 21: "Ten Ways to Organize Those Smallest of Items"

Chapter 22: "Recycle Those Unused Containers"

Organizing Challenge

* Organize your cosmetics, nail accessories, and hair accessories.

Chapter 21: "Cosmetics, Nail Accessories, and Hair Accessories"

Organizing Challenge

* Organize your family photos.

Chapter 13: "Computer Folders"

Chapter 21: "Pictures"

Organizing Challenge

* Get rid of any movies and music you no longer watch or listen to.

Chapter 21: "Movies, DVDs, Music, and CDs"

Organizing Challenge

* Straighten out the hanging cords behind your desk.

Chapter 21: "Taming Your Cords and Wires"

Organizing Challenge

* Update your contact sheet, Rolodex, address book, cell phone, and email contact information.

Chapter 11: "Think Ahead, Plan Ahead"

Chapter 15: "Leaving Your Children Home Alone"

Chapter 21: "Replace That Rolodex"

Organizing Challenge

* Clean out and organize your garage.

> **Chapter 2**: "The ABC's of Organization"
>
> **Chapter 3**: "Pick a Number and Challenge Yourself"
>
> **Chapter 5**: "Adjustable Shelving"
>
> **Chapter 6**: "Visualize to Organize; See it, Find It"
>
> **Chapter 9**: "I Can't Remember Where I Put It!"
>
> **Chapter 21**: "Garage"

Organizing Challenge

* Find something to recycle and reuse that will help you organize a group of items.

> **Chapter 6**: "Keep It Stored Vertically"
>
> **Chapter 21**: "Ten Ways to Organize Those Smallest of Items"
>
> **Chapter 22**: "Recycle and Reuse"

Organizing Challenge

* Prep your next family calendar for the upcoming year. Add in special dates, events, and reminders.

> **Chapter 3**: "Focus on Areas of the Greatest Concern"
>
> **Chapter 6**: "Make it Stand Out With Colors"
>
> **Chapter 9**: "Don't Forget"
>
> **Chapter 9**: "Reminders"
>
> **Chapter 9**: "Remember to Pay Those Bills on Time!"

Chapter 11: "Family Calendar"

Chapter 14: "The Importance of Designating a Family Communication Area"

Chapter 21: "Medications"

Organizing Challenge

* Prepare for an emergency by creating an emergency kit for both your vehicle and your home. Make them both easily accessible.

Chapter 7: "Within Reach"

Chapter 11: "Think Ahead, Plan Ahead"

Chapter 11: "Do Before Leaving" and "Bring on Trip" Lists

Chapter 11: "Emergency Kits"

Chapter 14: "Post Important Information Where It Is Needed Most"

Chapter 15: "Leaving Your Children Home Alone"

Organizing Challenge

* Get your final affairs in order.

Chapter 11: "Final Affairs in Order"

Organizing Challenge

* Find ten drinking glasses, cups or coffee mugs to throw out.

Chapter 3: "Pick a Number and Challenge Yourself"

Chapter 8: "How Many Can You Get Rid Of?"

Chapter 22: "What Can You Recycle?"

Write in your personal challenges here:

_____

_____

_____

_____

_____

_____

_____

_____

_____

_____

_____

_____

_____

Conclusion

Once you have organized as much as possible, take time to enjoy the rewards of being organized. Remember to take a few minutes every day to maintain everything you have done. Continue to clear out developing clutter, return items to their proper place, and if necessary make new areas for new items that need a home. The results will simply amaze you!

About Christina Scalise

Christina Scalise is a Professional Organizer, author, wife and mother of three. She resides in upstate New York with her family and is the author of *Organize Your Finances, Your Kids, Your Life!* and *Organize Your Life And More.* She also writes many articles, and provides weekly tips and product recommendations on her website.

Additional Qualifications: Professional Organizer since 2004 (individual coaching for home and office), creator and owner of *Organize Your Life And More,* event organizer and planner, real estate management, business offices, town office management, and non-profit organizations.

www.OrganizeYourLifeAndMore.com